C-3632

CAREER EXAMINATIO

MW01672167

THIS IS YOUR **PASSBOOK**® FOR ...

COURT SECURITY SUPERVISOR

NLC®

NATIONAL LEARNING CORPORATION®

passbooks.com

COPYRIGHT NOTICE

NLC®

National Learning Corporation

212 Michael Drive, Syosset, NY 11791
(516) 921-8888 • www.passbooks.com
E-mail: info@passbooks.com

PUBLISHED IN THE UNITED STATES OF AMERICA

PASSBOOK® SERIES

THE *PASSBOOK® SERIES* has been created to prepare applicants and candidates for the ultimate academic battlefield – the examination room.

At some time in our lives, each and every one of us may be required to take an examination – for validation, matriculation, admission, qualification, registration, certification, or licensure.

Based on the assumption that every applicant or candidate has met the basic formal educational standards, has taken the required number of courses, and read the necessary texts, the *PASSBOOK® SERIES* furnishes the one special preparation which may assure passing with confidence, instead of failing with insecurity. Examination questions – together with answers – are furnished as the basic vehicle for study so that the mysteries of the examination and its compounding difficulties may be eliminated or diminished by a sure method.

This book is meant to help you pass your examination provided that you qualify and are serious in your objective.

The entire field is reviewed through the huge store of content information which is succinctly presented through a provocative and challenging approach – the question-and-answer method.

A climate of success is established by furnishing the correct answers at the end of each test.

You soon learn to recognize types of questions, forms of questions, and patterns of questioning. You may even begin to anticipate expected outcomes.

You perceive that many questions are repeated or adapted so that you can gain acute insights, which may enable you to score many sure points.

You learn how to confront new questions, or types of questions, and to attack them confidently and work out the correct answers.

You note objectives and emphases, and recognize pitfalls and dangers, so that you may make positive educational adjustments.

Moreover, you are kept fully informed in relation to new concepts, methods, practices, and directions in the field.

You discover that you arre actually taking the examination all the time: you are preparing for the examination by "taking" an examination, not by reading extraneous and/or supererogatory textbooks.

In short, this PASSBOOK®, used directedly, should be an important factor in helping you to pass your test.

COURT SECURITY SUPERVISOR

DUTIES
Oversees and is responsible for the day to day operations of the Court Security Unit; monitors assignment and transfer of Court Security personnel; reviews employees evaluations; performs a variety of other related tasks as required.

SUBJECT OF EXAMINATION
The written test will cover knowledge, skills, and/or abilities in such areas as:

1. Reasoning clearly and making sound judgments related to the provision of security in courtroom situation;
2. Legal terminology, documents and forms;
3. Evaluating information and evidence;
4. Supervision;
5. Understanding and interpreting written material; and
6. Preparation of written material.

HOW TO TAKE A TEST

I. YOU MUST PASS AN EXAMINATION

A. WHAT EVERY CANDIDATE SHOULD KNOW

Examination applicants often ask us for help in preparing for the written test. What can I study in advance? What kinds of questions will be asked? How will the test be given? How will the papers be graded?

As an applicant for a civil service examination, you may be wondering about some of these things. Our purpose here is to suggest effective methods of advance study and to describe civil service examinations.

Your chances for success on this examination can be increased if you know how to prepare. Those "pre-examination jitters" can be reduced if you know what to expect. You can even experience an adventure in good citizenship if you know why civil service exams are given.

B. WHY ARE CIVIL SERVICE EXAMINATIONS GIVEN?

Civil service examinations are important to you in two ways. As a citizen, you want public jobs filled by employees who know how to do their work. As a job seeker, you want a fair chance to compete for that job on an equal footing with other candidates. The best-known means of accomplishing this two-fold goal is the competitive examination.

Exams are widely publicized throughout the nation. They may be administered for jobs in federal, state, city, municipal, town or village governments or agencies.

Any citizen may apply, with some limitations, such as the age or residence of applicants. Your experience and education may be reviewed to see whether you meet the requirements for the particular examination. When these requirements exist, they are reasonable and applied consistently to all applicants. Thus, a competitive examination may cause you some uneasiness now, but it is your privilege and safeguard.

C. HOW ARE CIVIL SERVICE EXAMS DEVELOPED?

Examinations are carefully written by trained technicians who are specialists in the field known as "psychological measurement," in consultation with recognized authorities in the field of work that the test will cover. These experts recommend the subject matter areas or skills to be tested; only those knowledges or skills important to your success on the job are included. The most reliable books and source materials available are used as references. Together, the experts and technicians judge the difficulty level of the questions.

Test technicians know how to phrase questions so that the problem is clearly stated. Their ethics do not permit "trick" or "catch" questions. Questions may have been tried out on sample groups, or subjected to statistical analysis, to determine their usefulness.

Written tests are often used in combination with performance tests, ratings of training and experience, and oral interviews. All of these measures combine to form the best-known means of finding the right person for the right job.

II. HOW TO PASS THE WRITTEN TEST

A. NATURE OF THE EXAMINATION

To prepare intelligently for civil service examinations, you should know how they differ from school examinations you have taken. In school you were assigned certain definite pages to read or subjects to cover. The examination questions were quite detailed and usually emphasized memory. Civil service exams, on the other hand, try to discover your present ability to perform the duties of a position, plus your potentiality to learn these duties. In other words, a civil service exam attempts to predict how successful you will be. Questions cover such a broad area that they cannot be as minute and detailed as school exam questions.

In the public service similar kinds of work, or positions, are grouped together in one "class." This process is known as *position-classification*. All the positions in a class are paid according to the salary range for that class. One class title covers all of these positions, and they are all tested by the same examination.

B. FOUR BASIC STEPS

1) Study the announcement

How, then, can you know what subjects to study? Our best answer is: "Learn as much as possible about the class of positions for which you've applied." The exam will test the knowledge, skills and abilities needed to do the work.

Your most valuable source of information about the position you want is the official exam announcement. This announcement lists the training and experience qualifications. Check these standards and apply only if you come reasonably close to meeting them.

The brief description of the position in the examination announcement offers some clues to the subjects which will be tested. Think about the job itself. Review the duties in your mind. Can you perform them, or are there some in which you are rusty? Fill in the blank spots in your preparation.

Many jurisdictions preview the written test in the exam announcement by including a section called "Knowledge and Abilities Required," "Scope of the Examination," or some similar heading. Here you will find out specifically what fields will be tested.

2) Review your own background

Once you learn in general what the position is all about, and what you need to know to do the work, ask yourself which subjects you already know fairly well and which need improvement. You may wonder whether to concentrate on improving your strong areas or on building some background in your fields of weakness. When the announcement has specified "some knowledge" or "considerable knowledge," or has used adjectives like "beginning principles of..." or "advanced ... methods," you can get a clue as to the number and difficulty of questions to be asked in any given field. More questions, and hence broader coverage, would be included for those subjects which are more important in the work. Now weigh your strengths and weaknesses against the job requirements and prepare accordingly.

3) Determine the level of the position

Another way to tell how intensively you should prepare is to understand the level of the job for which you are applying. Is it the entering level? In other words, is this the position in which beginners in a field of work are hired? Or is it an intermediate or advanced level? Sometimes this is indicated by such words as "Junior" or "Senior" in the class title. Other jurisdictions use Roman numerals to designate the level – Clerk I, Clerk II, for example. The word "Supervisor" sometimes appears in the title. If the level is not indicated by the title, check the description of duties. Will you be working under very close supervision, or will you have responsibility for independent decisions in this work?

4) Choose appropriate study materials

Now that you know the subjects to be examined and the relative amount of each subject to be covered, you can choose suitable study materials. For beginning level jobs, or even advanced ones, if you have a pronounced weakness in some aspect of your training, read a modern, standard textbook in that field. Be sure it is up to date and has general coverage. Such books are normally available at your library, and the librarian will be glad to help you locate one. For entry-level positions, questions of appropriate difficulty are chosen – neither highly advanced questions, nor those too simple. Such questions require careful thought but not advanced training.

If the position for which you are applying is technical or advanced, you will read more advanced, specialized material. If you are already familiar with the basic principles of your field, elementary textbooks would waste your time. Concentrate on advanced textbooks and technical periodicals. Think through the concepts and review difficult problems in your field.

These are all general sources. You can get more ideas on your own initiative, following these leads. For example, training manuals and publications of the government agency which employs workers in your field can be useful, particularly for technical and professional positions. A letter or visit to the government department involved may result in more specific study suggestions, and certainly will provide you with a more definite idea of the exact nature of the position you are seeking.

III. KINDS OF TESTS

Tests are used for purposes other than measuring knowledge and ability to perform specified duties. For some positions, it is equally important to test ability to make adjustments to new situations or to profit from training. In others, basic mental abilities not dependent on information are essential. Questions which test these things may not appear as pertinent to the duties of the position as those which test for knowledge and information. Yet they are often highly important parts of a fair examination. For very general questions, it is almost impossible to help you direct your study efforts. What we can do is to point out some of the more common of these general abilities needed in public service positions and describe some typical questions.

1) General information

Broad, general information has been found useful for predicting job success in some kinds of work. This is tested in a variety of ways, from vocabulary lists to questions about current events. Basic background in some field of work, such as sociology or economics, may be sampled in a group of questions. Often these are principles which have become familiar to most persons through exposure rather than through formal training. It is difficult to advise you how to study for these questions; being alert to the world around you is our best suggestion.

2) Verbal ability

An example of an ability needed in many positions is verbal or language ability. Verbal ability is, in brief, the ability to use and understand words. Vocabulary and grammar tests are typical measures of this ability. Reading comprehension or paragraph interpretation questions are common in many kinds of civil service tests. You are given a paragraph of written material and asked to find its central meaning.

3) Numerical ability

Number skills can be tested by the familiar arithmetic problem, by checking paired lists of numbers to see which are alike and which are different, or by interpreting charts and graphs. In the latter test, a graph may be printed in the test booklet which you are asked to use as the basis for answering questions.

4) Observation

A popular test for law-enforcement positions is the observation test. A picture is shown to you for several minutes, then taken away. Questions about the picture test your ability to observe both details and larger elements.

5) Following directions

In many positions in the public service, the employee must be able to carry out written instructions dependably and accurately. You may be given a chart with several columns, each column listing a variety of information. The questions require you to carry out directions involving the information given in the chart.

6) Skills and aptitudes

Performance tests effectively measure some manual skills and aptitudes. When the skill is one in which you are trained, such as typing or shorthand, you can practice. These tests are often very much like those given in business school or high school courses. For many of the other skills and aptitudes, however, no short-time preparation can be made. Skills and abilities natural to you or that you have developed throughout your lifetime are being tested.

Many of the general questions just described provide all the data needed to answer the questions and ask you to use your reasoning ability to find the answers. Your best preparation for these tests, as well as for tests of facts and ideas, is to be at your physical and mental best. You, no doubt, have your own methods of getting into an exam-taking mood and keeping "in shape." The next section lists some ideas on this subject.

IV. KINDS OF QUESTIONS

Only rarely is the "essay" question, which you answer in narrative form, used in civil service tests. Civil service tests are usually of the short-answer type. Full instructions for answering these questions will be given to you at the examination. But in case this is your first experience with short-answer questions and separate answer sheets, here is what you need to know:

1) Multiple-choice Questions

Most popular of the short-answer questions is the "multiple choice" or "best answer" question. It can be used, for example, to test for factual knowledge, ability to solve problems or judgment in meeting situations found at work.

A multiple-choice question is normally one of three types—

- It can begin with an incomplete statement followed by several possible endings. You are to find the one ending which *best* completes the statement, although some of the others may not be entirely wrong.
- It can also be a complete statement in the form of a question which is answered by choosing one of the statements listed.
- It can be in the form of a problem – again you select the best answer.

Here is an example of a multiple-choice question with a discussion which should give you some clues as to the method for choosing the right answer:

When an employee has a complaint about his assignment, the action which will *best* help him overcome his difficulty is to

A. discuss his difficulty with his coworkers
B. take the problem to the head of the organization
C. take the problem to the person who gave him the assignment
D. say nothing to anyone about his complaint

In answering this question, you should study each of the choices to find which is best. Consider choice "A" – Certainly an employee may discuss his complaint with fellow employees, but no change or improvement can result, and the complaint remains unresolved. Choice "B" is a poor choice since the head of the organization probably does not know what assignment you have been given, and taking your problem to him is known as "going over the head" of the supervisor. The supervisor, or person who made the assignment, is the person who can clarify it or correct any injustice. Choice "C" is, therefore, correct. To say nothing, as in choice "D," is unwise. Supervisors have and interest in knowing the problems employees are facing, and the employee is seeking a solution to his problem.

2) True/False Questions

The "true/false" or "right/wrong" form of question is sometimes used. Here a complete statement is given. Your job is to decide whether the statement is right or wrong.

SAMPLE: A roaming cell-phone call to a nearby city costs less than a non-roaming call to a distant city.

This statement is wrong, or false, since roaming calls are more expensive.

This is not a complete list of all possible question forms, although most of the others are variations of these common types. You will always get complete directions for answering questions. Be sure you understand *how* to mark your answers – ask questions until you do.

V. RECORDING YOUR ANSWERS

Computer terminals are used more and more today for many different kinds of exams.

For an examination with very few applicants, you may be told to record your answers in the test booklet itself. Separate answer sheets are much more common. If this separate answer sheet is to be scored by machine – and this is often the case – it is highly important that you mark your answers correctly in order to get credit.

An electronic scoring machine is often used in civil service offices because of the speed with which papers can be scored. Machine-scored answer sheets must be marked with a pencil, which will be given to you. This pencil has a high graphite content which responds to the electronic scoring machine. As a matter of fact, stray dots may register as answers, so do not let your pencil rest on the answer sheet while you are pondering the correct answer. Also, if your pencil lead breaks or is otherwise defective, ask for another.

Since the answer sheet will be dropped in a slot in the scoring machine, be careful not to bend the corners or get the paper crumpled.

The answer sheet normally has five vertical columns of numbers, with 30 numbers to a column. These numbers correspond to the question numbers in your test booklet. After each number, going across the page are four or five pairs of dotted lines. These short dotted lines have small letters or numbers above them. The first two pairs may also have a "T" or "F" above the letters. This indicates that the first two pairs only are to be used if the questions are of the true-false type. If the questions are multiple choice, disregard the "T" and "F" and pay attention only to the small letters or numbers.

Answer your questions in the manner of the sample that follows:

32. The largest city in the United States is
    - A. Washington, D.C.
    - B. New York City
    - C. Chicago
    - D. Detroit
    - E. San Francisco

1) Choose the answer you think is best. (New York City is the largest, so "B" is correct.)
2) Find the row of dotted lines numbered the same as the question you are answering. (Find row number 32)
3) Find the pair of dotted lines corresponding to the answer. (Find the pair of lines under the mark "B.")
4) Make a solid black mark between the dotted lines.

VI. BEFORE THE TEST

Common sense will help you find procedures to follow to get ready for an examination. Too many of us, however, overlook these sensible measures. Indeed, nervousness and fatigue have been found to be the most serious reasons why applicants fail to do their best on civil service tests. Here is a list of reminders:

- Begin your preparation early – Don't wait until the last minute to go scurrying around for books and materials or to find out what the position is all about.
- Prepare continuously – An hour a night for a week is better than an all-night cram session. This has been definitely established. What is more, a night a week for a month will return better dividends than crowding your study into a shorter period of time.
- Locate the place of the exam – You have been sent a notice telling you when and where to report for the examination. If the location is in a different town or otherwise unfamiliar to you, it would be well to inquire the best route and learn something about the building.
- Relax the night before the test – Allow your mind to rest. Do not study at all that night. Plan some mild recreation or diversion; then go to bed early and get a good night's sleep.
- Get up early enough to make a leisurely trip to the place for the test – This way unforeseen events, traffic snarls, unfamiliar buildings, etc. will not upset you.
- Dress comfortably – A written test is not a fashion show. You will be known by number and not by name, so wear something comfortable.
- Leave excess paraphernalia at home – Shopping bags and odd bundles will get in your way. You need bring only the items mentioned in the official notice you received; usually everything you need is provided. Do not bring reference books to the exam. They will only confuse those last minutes and be taken away from you when in the test room.
- Arrive somewhat ahead of time – If because of transportation schedules you must get there very early, bring a newspaper or magazine to take your mind off yourself while waiting.
- Locate the examination room – When you have found the proper room, you will be directed to the seat or part of the room where you will sit. Sometimes you are given a sheet of instructions to read while you are waiting. Do not fill out any forms until you are told to do so; just read them and be prepared.
- Relax and prepare to listen to the instructions
- If you have any physical problem that may keep you from doing your best, be sure to tell the test administrator. If you are sick or in poor health, you really cannot do your best on the exam. You can come back and take the test some other time.

VII. AT THE TEST

The day of the test is here and you have the test booklet in your hand. The temptation to get going is very strong. Caution! There is more to success than knowing the right answers. You must know how to identify your papers and understand variations in the type of short-answer question used in this particular examination. Follow these suggestions for maximum results from your efforts:

1) Cooperate with the monitor

The test administrator has a duty to create a situation in which you can be as much at ease as possible. He will give instructions, tell you when to begin, check to see that you are marking your answer sheet correctly, and so on. He is not there to guard you, although he will see that your competitors do not take unfair advantage. He wants to help you do your best.

2) Listen to all instructions

Don't jump the gun! Wait until you understand all directions. In most civil service tests you get more time than you need to answer the questions. So don't be in a hurry. Read each word of instructions until you clearly understand the meaning. Study the examples, listen to all announcements and follow directions. Ask questions if you do not understand what to do.

3) Identify your papers

Civil service exams are usually identified by number only. You will be assigned a number; you must not put your name on your test papers. Be sure to copy your number correctly. Since more than one exam may be given, copy your exact examination title.

4) Plan your time

Unless you are told that a test is a "speed" or "rate of work" test, speed itself is usually not important. Time enough to answer all the questions will be provided, but this does not mean that you have all day. An overall time limit has been set. Divide the total time (in minutes) by the number of questions to determine the approximate time you have for each question.

5) Do not linger over difficult questions

If you come across a difficult question, mark it with a paper clip (useful to have along) and come back to it when you have been through the booklet. One caution if you do this – be sure to skip a number on your answer sheet as well. Check often to be sure that you have not lost your place and that you are marking in the row numbered the same as the question you are answering.

6) Read the questions

Be sure you know what the question asks! Many capable people are unsuccessful because they failed to *read* the questions correctly.

7) Answer all questions

Unless you have been instructed that a penalty will be deducted for incorrect answers, it is better to guess than to omit a question.

8) Speed tests

It is often better NOT to guess on speed tests. It has been found that on timed tests people are tempted to spend the last few seconds before time is called in marking answers at random – without even reading them – in the hope of picking up a few extra points. To discourage this practice, the instructions may warn you that your score will be "corrected" for guessing. That is, a penalty will be applied. The incorrect answers will be deducted from the correct ones, or some other penalty formula will be used.

9) Review your answers

If you finish before time is called, go back to the questions you guessed or omitted to give them further thought. Review other answers if you have time.

10) Return your test materials

If you are ready to leave before others have finished or time is called, take ALL your materials to the monitor and leave quietly. Never take any test material with you. The monitor can discover whose papers are not complete, and taking a test booklet may be grounds for disqualification.

VIII. EXAMINATION TECHNIQUES

1) Read the general instructions carefully. These are usually printed on the first page of the exam booklet. As a rule, these instructions refer to the timing of the examination; the fact that you should not start work until the signal and must stop work at a signal, etc. If there are any *special* instructions, such as a choice of questions to be answered, make sure that you note this instruction carefully.

2) When you are ready to start work on the examination, that is as soon as the signal has been given, read the instructions to each question booklet, underline any key words or phrases, such as *least*, *best*, *outline*, *describe* and the like. In this way you will tend to answer as requested rather than discover on reviewing your paper that you *listed without describing*, that you selected the *worst* choice rather than the *best* choice, etc.

3) If the examination is of the objective or multiple-choice type – that is, each question will also give a series of possible answers: A, B, C or D, and you are called upon to select the best answer and write the letter next to that answer on your answer paper – it is advisable to start answering each question in turn. There may be anywhere from 50 to 100 such questions in the three or four hours allotted and you can see how much time would be taken if you read through all the questions before beginning to answer any. Furthermore, if you come across a question or group of questions which you know would be difficult to answer, it would undoubtedly affect your handling of all the other questions.

4) If the examination is of the essay type and contains but a few questions, it is a moot point as to whether you should read all the questions before starting to answer any one. Of course, if you are given a choice – say five out of seven and the like – then it is essential to read all the questions so you can eliminate the two that are most difficult. If, however, you are asked to answer all the questions, there may be danger in trying to answer the easiest one first because you may find that you will spend too much time on it. The best technique is to answer the first question, then proceed to the second, etc.

5) Time your answers. Before the exam begins, write down the time it started, then add the time allowed for the examination and write down the time it must be completed, then divide the time available somewhat as follows:

- If 3-1/2 hours are allowed, that would be 210 minutes. If you have 80 objective-type questions, that would be an average of 2-1/2 minutes per question. Allow yourself no more than 2 minutes per question, or a total of 160 minutes, which will permit about 50 minutes to review.
- If for the time allotment of 210 minutes there are 7 essay questions to answer, that would average about 30 minutes a question. Give yourself only 25 minutes per question so that you have about 35 minutes to review.

6) The most important instruction is to *read each question* and make sure you know what is wanted. The second most important instruction is to *time yourself properly* so that you answer every question. The third most important instruction is to *answer every question*. Guess if you have to but include something for each question. Remember that you will receive no credit for a blank and will probably receive some credit if you write something in answer to an essay question. If you guess a letter – say "B" for a multiple-choice question – you may have guessed right. If you leave a blank as an answer to a multiple-choice question, the examiners may respect your feelings but it will not add a point to your score. Some exams may penalize you for wrong answers, so in such cases *only*, you may not want to guess unless you have some basis for your answer.

7) Suggestions
   a. Objective-type questions
      1. Examine the question booklet for proper sequence of pages and questions
      2. Read all instructions carefully
      3. Skip any question which seems too difficult; return to it after all other questions have been answered
      4. Apportion your time properly; do not spend too much time on any single question or group of questions
      5. Note and underline key words – *all, most, fewest, least, best, worst, same, opposite,* etc.
      6. Pay particular attention to negatives
      7. Note unusual option, e.g., unduly long, short, complex, different or similar in content to the body of the question
      8. Observe the use of "hedging" words – *probably, may, most likely,* etc.
      9. Make sure that your answer is put next to the same number as the question
      10. Do not second-guess unless you have good reason to believe the second answer is definitely more correct
      11. Cross out original answer if you decide another answer is more accurate; do not erase until you are ready to hand your paper in
      12. Answer all questions; guess unless instructed otherwise
      13. Leave time for review

   b. Essay questions
      1. Read each question carefully
      2. Determine exactly what is wanted. Underline key words or phrases.
      3. Decide on outline or paragraph answer

4. Include many different points and elements unless asked to develop any one or two points or elements
5. Show impartiality by giving pros and cons unless directed to select one side only
6. Make and write down any assumptions you find necessary to answer the questions
7. Watch your English, grammar, punctuation and choice of words
8. Time your answers; don't crowd material

8) Answering the essay question

Most essay questions can be answered by framing the specific response around several key words or ideas. Here are a few such key words or ideas:

M's: manpower, materials, methods, money, management
P's: purpose, program, policy, plan, procedure, practice, problems, pitfalls, personnel, public relations

a. Six basic steps in handling problems:
   1. Preliminary plan and background development
   2. Collect information, data and facts
   3. Analyze and interpret information, data and facts
   4. Analyze and develop solutions as well as make recommendations
   5. Prepare report and sell recommendations
   6. Install recommendations and follow up effectiveness

b. Pitfalls to avoid
   1. *Taking things for granted* – A statement of the situation does not necessarily imply that each of the elements is necessarily true; for example, a complaint may be invalid and biased so that all that can be taken for granted is that a complaint has been registered
   2. *Considering only one side of a situation* – Wherever possible, indicate several alternatives and then point out the reasons you selected the best one
   3. *Failing to indicate follow up* – Whenever your answer indicates action on your part, make certain that you will take proper follow-up action to see how successful your recommendations, procedures or actions turn out to be
   4. *Taking too long in answering any single question* – Remember to time your answers properly

IX. AFTER THE TEST

Scoring procedures differ in detail among civil service jurisdictions although the general principles are the same. Whether the papers are hand-scored or graded by machine we have described, they are nearly always graded by number. That is, the person who marks the paper knows only the number – never the name – of the applicant. Not until all the papers have been graded will they be matched with names. If other tests, such as training and experience or oral interview ratings have been given, scores will be combined. Different parts of the examination usually have different weights. For example, the written test might count 60 percent of the final grade, and a rating of training and experience 40 percent. In many jurisdictions, veterans will have a certain number of points added to their grades.

After the final grade has been determined, the names are placed in grade order and an eligible list is established. There are various methods for resolving ties between those who get the same final grade – probably the most common is to place first the name of the person whose application was received first. Job offers are made from the eligible list in the order the names appear on it. You will be notified of your grade and your rank as soon as all these computations have been made. This will be done as rapidly as possible.

People who are found to meet the requirements in the announcement are called "eligibles." Their names are put on a list of eligible candidates. An eligible's chances of getting a job depend on how high he stands on this list and how fast agencies are filling jobs from the list.

When a job is to be filled from a list of eligibles, the agency asks for the names of people on the list of eligibles for that job. When the civil service commission receives this request, it sends to the agency the names of the three people highest on this list. Or, if the job to be filled has specialized requirements, the office sends the agency the names of the top three persons who meet these requirements from the general list.

The appointing officer makes a choice from among the three people whose names were sent to him. If the selected person accepts the appointment, the names of the others are put back on the list to be considered for future openings.

That is the rule in hiring from all kinds of eligible lists, whether they are for typist, carpenter, chemist, or something else. For every vacancy, the appointing officer has his choice of any one of the top three eligibles on the list. This explains why the person whose name is on top of the list sometimes does not get an appointment when some of the persons lower on the list do. If the appointing officer chooses the second or third eligible, the No. 1 eligible does not get a job at once, but stays on the list until he is appointed or the list is terminated.

X. HOW TO PASS THE INTERVIEW TEST

The examination for which you applied requires an oral interview test. You have already taken the written test and you are now being called for the interview test – the final part of the formal examination.

You may think that it is not possible to prepare for an interview test and that there are no procedures to follow during an interview. Our purpose is to point out some things you can do in advance that will help you and some good rules to follow and pitfalls to avoid while you are being interviewed.

What is an interview supposed to test?

The written examination is designed to test the technical knowledge and competence of the candidate; the oral is designed to evaluate intangible qualities, not readily measured otherwise, and to establish a list showing the relative fitness of each candidate – as measured against his competitors – for the position sought. Scoring is not on the basis of "right" and "wrong," but on a sliding scale of values ranging from "not passable" to "outstanding." As a matter of fact, it is possible to achieve a relatively low score without a single "incorrect" answer because of evident weakness in the qualities being measured.

Occasionally, an examination may consist entirely of an oral test – either an individual or a group oral. In such cases, information is sought concerning the technical knowledges and abilities of the candidate, since there has been no written examination for this purpose. More commonly, however, an oral test is used to supplement a written examination.

Who conducts interviews?

The composition of oral boards varies among different jurisdictions. In nearly all, a representative of the personnel department serves as chairman. One of the members of the board may be a representative of the department in which the candidate would work. In some cases, "outside experts" are used, and, frequently, a businessman or some other representative of the general public is asked to serve. Labor and management or other special groups may be represented. The aim is to secure the services of experts in the appropriate field.

However the board is composed, it is a good idea (and not at all improper or unethical) to ascertain in advance of the interview who the members are and what groups they represent. When you are introduced to them, you will have some idea of their backgrounds and interests, and at least you will not stutter and stammer over their names.

What should be done before the interview?

While knowledge about the board members is useful and takes some of the surprise element out of the interview, there is other preparation which is more substantive. It *is* possible to prepare for an oral interview – in several ways:

1) Keep a copy of your application and review it carefully before the interview

This may be the only document before the oral board, and the starting point of the interview. Know what education and experience you have listed there, and the sequence and dates of all of it. Sometimes the board will ask you to review the highlights of your experience for them; you should not have to hem and haw doing it.

2) Study the class specification and the examination announcement

Usually, the oral board has one or both of these to guide them. The qualities, characteristics or knowledges required by the position sought are stated in these documents. They offer valuable clues as to the nature of the oral interview. For example, if the job involves supervisory responsibilities, the announcement will usually indicate that knowledge of modern supervisory methods and the qualifications of the candidate as a supervisor will be tested. If so, you can expect such questions, frequently in the form of a hypothetical situation which you are expected to solve. NEVER go into an oral without knowledge of the duties and responsibilities of the job you seek.

3) Think through each qualification required

Try to visualize the kind of questions you would ask if you were a board member. How well could you answer them? Try especially to appraise your own knowledge and background in each area, *measured against the job sought*, and identify any areas in which you are weak. Be critical and realistic – do not flatter yourself.

4) Do some general reading in areas in which you feel you may be weak

For example, if the job involves supervision and your past experience has NOT, some general reading in supervisory methods and practices, particularly in the field of human relations, might be useful. Do NOT study agency procedures or detailed manuals. The oral board will be testing your understanding and capacity, not your memory.

5) Get a good night's sleep and watch your general health and mental attitude

You will want a clear head at the interview. Take care of a cold or any other minor ailment, and of course, no hangovers.

What should be done on the day of the interview?

Now comes the day of the interview itself. Give yourself plenty of time to get there. Plan to arrive somewhat ahead of the scheduled time, particularly if your appointment is in the fore part of the day. If a previous candidate fails to appear, the board might be ready for you a bit early. By early afternoon an oral board is almost invariably behind schedule if there are many candidates, and you may have to wait. Take along a book or magazine to read, or your application to review, but leave any extraneous material in the waiting room when you go in for your interview. In any event, relax and compose yourself.

The matter of dress is important. The board is forming impressions about you – from your experience, your manners, your attitude, and your appearance. Give your personal appearance careful attention. Dress your best, but not your flashiest. Choose conservative, appropriate clothing, and be sure it is immaculate. This is a business interview, and your appearance should indicate that you regard it as such. Besides, being well groomed and properly dressed will help boost your confidence.

Sooner or later, someone will call your name and escort you into the interview room. *This is it.* From here on you are on your own. It is too late for any more preparation. But remember, you asked for this opportunity to prove your fitness, and you are here because your request was granted.

What happens when you go in?

The usual sequence of events will be as follows: The clerk (who is often the board stenographer) will introduce you to the chairman of the oral board, who will introduce you to the other members of the board. Acknowledge the introductions before you sit down. Do not be surprised if you find a microphone facing you or a stenotypist sitting by. Oral interviews are usually recorded in the event of an appeal or other review.

Usually the chairman of the board will open the interview by reviewing the highlights of your education and work experience from your application – primarily for the benefit of the other members of the board, as well as to get the material into the record. Do not interrupt or comment unless there is an error or significant misinterpretation; if that is the case, do not hesitate. But do not quibble about insignificant matters. Also, he will usually ask you some question about your education, experience or your present job – partly to get you to start talking and to establish the interviewing "rapport." He may start the actual questioning, or turn it over to one of the other members. Frequently, each member undertakes the questioning on a particular area, one in which he is perhaps most competent, so you can expect each member to participate in the examination. Because time is limited, you may also expect some rather abrupt switches in the direction the questioning takes, so do not be upset by it. Normally, a board member will not pursue a single line of questioning unless he discovers a particular strength or weakness.

After each member has participated, the chairman will usually ask whether any member has any further questions, then will ask you if you have anything you wish to add. Unless you are expecting this question, it may floor you. Worse, it may start you off on an extended, extemporaneous speech. The board is not usually seeking more information. The question is principally to offer you a last opportunity to present further qualifications or to indicate that you have nothing to add. So, if you feel that a significant qualification or characteristic has been overlooked, it is proper to point it out in a sentence or so. Do not compliment the board on the thoroughness of their examination – they have been sketchy, and you know it. If you wish, merely say, "No thank you, I have nothing further to add." This is a point where you can "talk yourself out" of a good impression or fail to present an important bit of information. Remember, *you close the interview yourself.*

The chairman will then say, "That is all, Mr. ______, thank you." Do not be startled; the interview is over, and quicker than you think. Thank him, gather your belongings and take your leave. Save your sigh of relief for the other side of the door.

How to put your best foot forward

Throughout this entire process, you may feel that the board individually and collectively is trying to pierce your defenses, seek out your hidden weaknesses and embarrass and confuse you. Actually, this is not true. They are obliged to make an appraisal of your qualifications for the job you are seeking, and they want to see you in your best light. Remember, they must interview all candidates and a non-cooperative candidate may become a failure in spite of their best efforts to bring out his qualifications. Here are 15 suggestions that will help you:

1) Be natural – Keep your attitude confident, not cocky

If you are not confident that you can do the job, do not expect the board to be. Do not apologize for your weaknesses, try to bring out your strong points. The board is interested in a positive, not negative, presentation. Cockiness will antagonize any board member and make him wonder if you are covering up a weakness by a false show of strength.

2) Get comfortable, but don't lounge or sprawl

Sit erectly but not stiffly. A careless posture may lead the board to conclude that you are careless in other things, or at least that you are not impressed by the importance of the occasion. Either conclusion is natural, even if incorrect. Do not fuss with your clothing, a pencil or an ashtray. Your hands may occasionally be useful to emphasize a point; do not let them become a point of distraction.

3) Do not wisecrack or make small talk

This is a serious situation, and your attitude should show that you consider it as such. Further, the time of the board is limited – they do not want to waste it, and neither should you.

4) Do not exaggerate your experience or abilities

In the first place, from information in the application or other interviews and sources, the board may know more about you than you think. Secondly, you probably will not get away with it. An experienced board is rather adept at spotting such a situation, so do not take the chance.

5) If you know a board member, do not make a point of it, yet do not hide it

Certainly you are not fooling him, and probably not the other members of the board. Do not try to take advantage of your acquaintanceship – it will probably do you little good.

6) Do not dominate the interview

Let the board do that. They will give you the clues – do not assume that you have to do all the talking. Realize that the board has a number of questions to ask you, and do not try to take up all the interview time by showing off your extensive knowledge of the answer to the first one.

7) Be attentive

You only have 20 minutes or so, and you should keep your attention at its sharpest throughout. When a member is addressing a problem or question to you, give him your undivided attention. Address your reply principally to him, but do not exclude the other board members.

8) Do not interrupt

A board member may be stating a problem for you to analyze. He will ask you a question when the time comes. Let him state the problem, and wait for the question.

9) Make sure you understand the question

Do not try to answer until you are sure what the question is. If it is not clear, restate it in your own words or ask the board member to clarify it for you. However, do not haggle about minor elements.

10) Reply promptly but not hastily

A common entry on oral board rating sheets is "candidate responded readily," or "candidate hesitated in replies." Respond as promptly and quickly as you can, but do not jump to a hasty, ill-considered answer.

11) Do not be peremptory in your answers

A brief answer is proper – but do not fire your answer back. That is a losing game from your point of view. The board member can probably ask questions much faster than you can answer them.

12) Do not try to create the answer you think the board member wants

He is interested in what kind of mind you have and how it works – not in playing games. Furthermore, he can usually spot this practice and will actually grade you down on it.

13) Do not switch sides in your reply merely to agree with a board member

Frequently, a member will take a contrary position merely to draw you out and to see if you are willing and able to defend your point of view. Do not start a debate, yet do not surrender a good position. If a position is worth taking, it is worth defending.

14) Do not be afraid to admit an error in judgment if you are shown to be wrong

The board knows that you are forced to reply without any opportunity for careful consideration. Your answer may be demonstrably wrong. If so, admit it and get on with the interview.

15) Do not dwell at length on your present job

The opening question may relate to your present assignment. Answer the question but do not go into an extended discussion. You are being examined for a *new* job, not your present one. As a matter of fact, try to phrase ALL your answers in terms of the job for which you are being examined.

Basis of Rating

Probably you will forget most of these "do's" and "don'ts" when you walk into the oral interview room. Even remembering them all will not ensure you a passing grade. Perhaps you did not have the qualifications in the first place. But remembering them will help you to put your best foot forward, without treading on the toes of the board members.

Rumor and popular opinion to the contrary notwithstanding, an oral board wants you to make the best appearance possible. They know you are under pressure – but they also want to see how you respond to it as a guide to what your reaction would be under the pressures of the job you seek. They will be influenced by the degree of poise you display, the personal traits you show and the manner in which you respond.

ABOUT THIS BOOK

This book contains tests divided into Examination Sections. Go through each test, answering every question in the margin. At the end of each test look at the answer key and check your answers. On the ones you got wrong, look at the right answer choice and learn. Do not fill in the answers first. Do not memorize the questions and answers, but understand the answer and principles involved. On your test, the questions will likely be different from the samples. Questions are changed and new ones added. If you understand these past questions you should have success with any changes that arise. Tests may consist of several types of questions. We have additional books on each subject should more study be advisable or necessary for you. Finally, the more you study, the better prepared you will be. This book is intended to be the last thing you study before you walk into the examination room. Prior study of relevant texts is also recommended. NLC publishes some of these in our Fundamental Series. Knowledge and good sense are important factors in passing your exam. Good luck also helps. So now study this Passbook, absorb the material contained within and take that knowledge into the examination. Then do your best to pass that exam.

EXAMINATION SECTION

EXAMINATION SECTION
TEST 1

DIRECTIONS: Each question or incomplete statement is followed by several suggested answers or completions. Select the one that BEST answers the question or completes the statement. *PRINT THE LETTER OF THE CORRECT ANSWER IN THE SPACE AT THE RIGHT.*

1. Physical and mental health are essential to the officer. According to this statement, the officer MUST be 1._____

   A. as wise as he is strong
   B. smarter than most people
   C. sound in mind and body
   D. stronger than the average criminal

2. Teamwork is the basis of successful law enforcement. The factor stressed by this statement is 2._____

   A. cooperation B. determination
   C. initiative D. pride

3. Legal procedure is a means, not an end. Its function is merely to accomplish the enforcement of legal rights. 3._____
   A litigant has no vested interest in the observance of the rules of procedure as such. All that he should be entitled to demand is that he be given an opportunity for a fair and impartial trial of his case. He should not be permitted to invoke the aid of technical rules merely to embarrass his adversary.
   According to this paragraph, it is MOST correct to state that

   A. observance of the rules of procedure guarantees a fair trial
   B. embarrassment of an adversary through technical rules does not make a fair trial
   C. a litigant is not interested in the observance of rules of procedure
   D. technical rules must not be used in a trial

4. One theory states that all criminal behavior is taught by a process of communication within small intimate groups. An individual engages in criminal behavior if the number of criminal patterns which he has acquired exceed the number of non-criminal patterns. 4._____
   This statement indicates that criminal behavior is

   A. learned B. instinctive
   C. hereditary D. reprehensible

5. The law enforcement staff of today requires training and mental qualities of a high order. The poorly or partially prepared staff member lowers the standard of work, retards his own earning power, and fails in a career meant to provide a livelihood and social improvement. 5._____
   According to this statement,

   A. an inefficient member of a law enforcement staff will still earn a good livelihood
   B. law enforcement officers move in good social circles
   C. many people fail in law enforcement careers
   D. persons of training and ability are essential to a law enforcement staff

6. In any state, no crime can occur unless there is a written law forbidding the act or the omission in question; and even though an act may not be exactly in harmony with public policy, such act is not a crime unless it is expressly forbidden by legislative statement. According to the above statement, 6.____

A. a crime is committed with reference to a particular law
B. acts not in harmony with public policy should be forbidden by law
C. non-criminal activity will promote public welfare
D. legislative enactments frequently forbid actions in harmony with public policy

7. The unrestricted sale of firearms is one of the main causes of our shameful crime record. According to this statement, one of the causes of our crime record is 7.____

A. development of firepower
B. ease of securing weapons
C. increased skill in using guns
D. scientific perfection of firearms

8. Every person must be informed of the reason for his arrest unless he is arrested in the actual commission of a crime. Sufficient force to effect the arrest may be used, but the courts frown on brutal methods.
According to this statement, a person does not have to be informed of the reason for his arrest if 8.____

A. brutal force was not used in effecting it
B. the courts will later turn the defendant loose
C. the person arrested knows force will be used if necessary
D. the reason for it is clearly evident from the circumstances

9. An important duty of an officer is to keep order in the court.
On the basis of this statement, it is PROBABLY true that 9.____

A. it is more important for an officer to be strong than it is for him to be smart
B. people involved in court trials are noisy if not kept in check
C. not every duty of an officer is important
D. the maintenance of order is important for the proper conduct of court business

10. Ideally, a correctional system should include several types of institutions to provide different degrees of custody.
On the basis of this statement, one could MOST reasonably say that 10.____

A. as the number of institutions in a correctional system increases, the efficiency of the system increases
B. the difference in degree of custody for the inmate depends on the types of institutions in a correctional system
C. the greater the variety of institutions, the stricter the degree of custody that can be maintained
D. the same type of correctional institution is not desirable for the custody of all prisoners

11. The enforced idleness of a large percentage of adult men and women in our prisons is one of the direct causes of the tensions which burst forth in riot and disorder. 11.____
On the basis of this statement, a good reason why inmates should perform daily work of some kind is that

A. better morale and discipline can be maintained when inmates are kept busy
B. daily work is an effective way of punishing inmates for the crimes they have committed
C. law-abiding citizens must work, therefore labor should also be required of inmates
D. products of inmates' labor will in part pay the cost of their maintenance

12. With industry invading rural areas, the use of the automobile, and the speed of modern communications and transportation, the problems of neglect and delinquency are no longer peculiar to cities but an established feature of everyday life. 12.____
This statement implies MOST directly that

A. delinquents are moving from cities to rural areas
B. delinquency and neglect are found in rural areas
C. delinquency is not as much of a problem in rural areas as in cities
D. rural areas now surpass cities in industry

13. Young men from minority groups, if unable to find employment, become discouraged and hopeless because of their economic position and may finally resort to any means of supplying their wants. 13.____
The MOST reasonable of the following conclusions that may be drawn from this statement only is that

A. discouragement sometimes leads to crime
B. in general, young men from minority groups are criminals
C. unemployment turns young men from crime
D. young men from minority groups are seldom employed

14. To prevent crime, we must deal with the possible criminal long before he reaches the prison. Our aim should be not merely to reform the law breakers but to strike at the roots of crime: neglectful parents, bad companions, unsatisfactory homes, selfishness, disregard for the rights of others, and bad social conditions. 14.____
The above statement recommends

A. abolition of prisons
B. better reformatories
C. compulsory education
D. general social reform

15. There is evidence which shows that comic books which glorify the criminal and criminal acts have a distinct influence in producing young criminals. 15.____
According to this statement,

A. comic books affect the development of criminal careers
B. comic books specialize in reporting criminal acts
C. young criminals read comic books exclusively
D. young criminals should not be permitted to read comic books

16. Suppose a study shows that juvenile delinquents are equal in intelligence but three school grades behind juvenile non-delinquents. 16.____
On the basis of this information only, it is MOST reasonable to say that

A. a delinquent usually progresses to the educational limit set by his intelligence
B. educational achievement depends on intelligence only
C. educational achievement is closely associated with delinquency
D. lack of intelligence is closely associated with delinquency

17. There is no proof today that the experience of a prison sentence makes a better citizen of an adult. On the contrary, there seems some evidence that the experience is an unwholesome one that frequently confirms the criminality of the inmate. 17.____
From the above paragraph only, it may be BEST concluded that

A. prison sentences tend to punish rather than rehabilitate
B. all criminals should be given prison sentences
C. we should abandon our penal institutions
D. penal institutions are effective in rehabilitating criminals

18. Some courts are referred to as *criminal* courts while others are known as *civil* courts. 18.____
This distinction in name is MOST probably based on the

A. historical origin of the court
B. link between the court and the police
C. manner in which the judges are chosen
D. type of cases tried there

19. Many children who are exposed to contacts and experiences of a delinquent nature become educated and trained in crime in the course of participating in the daily life of the neighborhood. 19.____
From this statement only, we may reasonably conclude that

A. delinquency passes from parent to child
B. neighborhood influences are usually bad
C. schools are training grounds for delinquents
D. none of the above conclusions is reasonable

20. Old age insurance, for whose benefits a quarter of a million city employees may elect to become eligible, is one feature of the Social Security Act that is wholly administered by the Federal government. 20.____
On the basis of this paragraph only, it may MOST reasonably be inferred that

A. a quarter of a million city employees are drawing old age insurance
B. a quarter of a million city employees have elected to become eligible for old age insurance
C. the city has no part in administering Social Security old age insurance
D. only the Federal government administers the Social Security Act

21. An officer's revolver is a defensive, and not offensive, weapon. 21.____
On the basis of this statement only, an officer should BEST draw his revolver to

A. fire at an unarmed burglar
B. force a suspect to confess
C. frighten a juvenile delinquent
D. protect his own life

22. Prevention of crime is of greater value to the community than the punishment of crime. If this statement is accepted as true, GREATEST emphasis should be placed on 22.____

A. malingering
B. medication
C. imprisonment
D. rehabilitation

23. The criminal is rarely or never reformed. Acceptance of this statement as true would mean that GREATEST emphasis should be placed on 23.____

A. imprisonment
B. parole
C. probation
D. malingering

24. The MOST accurate of the following statements about persons convicted of crimes is that 24.____

A. their criminal behavior is almost invariably the result of low intelligence
B. they are almost invariably legally insane
C. they are more likely to come from underprivileged groups than from other groups
D. they have certain facial characteristics which distinguish them from non-criminals

25. Suppose a study shows that the I.Q. (Intelligence Quotient) of prison inmates is 95 as opposed to an I.Q. of 100 for a numerically equivalent civilian group. A claim, on the basis of this study, that criminals have a lower I.Q. than non-criminals would be 25.____

A. *improper;* prison inmates are criminals who have been caught
B. *proper;* the study was numerically well done
C. *improper;* the sample was inadequate
D. *proper;* even misdemeanors are sometimes penalized by prison sentences

Questions 26-45.

DIRECTIONS: Select the number of the word or expression that MOST NEARLY expresses the meaning of the capitalized word in the group.

26. ABDUCT 26.____

A. lead B. kidnap C. sudden D. worthless

27. BIAS 27.____

A. ability B. envy C. prejudice D. privilege

28. COERCE 28.____

A. cancel B. force C. rescind D. rugged

29. CONDONE 29.____

A. combine B. pardon C. revive D. spice

30. CONSISTENCY 30.____

A. bravery
B. readiness
C. strain
D. uniformity

31. CREDENCE 31.____

A. belief
B. devotion
C. resemblance
D. tempo

32. CURRENT 32.____

A. backward
B. brave
C. prevailing
D. wary

33. CUSTODY 33.____

A. advisement
B. belligerence
C. guardianship
D. suspicion

34. DEBILITY 34.____

A. deceitfulness
B. decency
C. strength
D. weakness

35. DEPLETE 35.____

A. beg B. empty C. excuse D. fold

36. ENUMERATE 36.____

A. name one by one
B. disappear
C. get rid of
D. pretend

37. FEIGN 37.____

A. allow B. incur C. pretend D. weaken

38. INSTIGATE 38.____

A. analyze
B. coordinate
C. oppose
D. provoke

39. LIABLE 39.____

A. careless
B. growing
C. mistaken
D. responsible

40. PONDER 40.____

A. attack B. heavy C. meditate D. solicit

41. PUGILIST 41.____

A. farmer
B. politician
C. prize fighter
D. stage actor

42. QUELL 42.____

A. explode B. inform C. shake D. suppress

43. RECIPROCAL 43.____

A. mutual
B. organized
C. redundant
D. thoughtful

44. RUSE 44.____

A. burn B. impolite C. rot D. trick

45. STEALTHY 45.____

A. crazed B. flowing C. sly D. wicked

Questions 46-50.

DIRECTIONS: Each of the sentences in Questions 46 through 50 may be classified under one of the following four categories:

A. faulty because of incorrect grammar
B. faulty because of incorrect punctuation
C. faulty because of incorrect capitalization or incorrect spelling
D. correct

Examine each sentence carefully to determine under which of the above four options it is best classified. Then, in the space at the right, print the capital letter preceding the option which is the BEST of the four suggested above. Each faulty sentence contains but one type of error. Consider a sentence to be correct if it contains none of the types of errors mentioned, even though there may be other correct ways of expressing the same thought.

46. They told both he and I that the prisoner had escaped. 46.____

47. Any superior officer, who, disregards the just complaints of his subordinates, is remiss in the performance of his duty. 47.____

48. Only those members of the national organization who resided in the Middle west attended the conference in Chicago. 48.____

49. We told him to give the investigation assignment to whoever was available. 49.____

50. Please do not disappoint and embarass us by not appearing in court. 50.____

KEY (CORRECT ANSWERS)

1. C	11. A	21. D	31. A	41. C
2. A	12. B	22. D	32. C	42. D
3. B	13. A	23. A	33. C	43. A
4. A	14. D	24. C	34. D	44. D
5. D	15. A	25. A	35. B	45. C
6. A	16. C	26. B	36. A	46. A
7. B	17. A	27. C	37. C	47. B
8. D	18. D	28. B	38. D	48. C
9. D	19. D	29. B	39. D	49. D
10. D	20. C	30. D	40. C	50. C

TEST 2

DIRECTIONS: Each question or incomplete statement is followed by several suggested answers or completions. Select the one that BEST answers the question or completes the statement. *PRINT THE LETTER OF THE CORRECT ANSWER IN THE SPACE AT THE RIGHT.*

1. Suppose a man falls from a two-story high scaffold and is unconscious. You should 1.____

   A. call for medical assistance and avoid moving the man
   B. get someone to help you move him indoors to a bed
   C. have someone help you walk him around until he revives
   D. hold his head up and pour a stimulant down his throat

2. For proper first aid treatment, a person who has fainted should be 2.____

   A. doused with cold water and then warmly covered
   B. given artificial respiration until he is revived
   C. laid down with his head lower than the rest of his body
   D. slapped on the face until he is revived

3. If you are called on to give first aid to a person who is suffering from shock, you should 3.____

   A. apply cold towels
   B. give him a stimulant
   C. keep him awake
   D. wrap him warmly

4. Artificial respiration would NOT be proper first aid for a person suffering from 4.____

   A. drowning
   B. electric shock
   C. external bleeding
   D. suffocation

5. Suppose you are called on to give first aid to several victims of an accident. First attention should be given to the one who is 5.____

   A. bleeding severely
   B. groaning loudly
   C. unconscious
   D. vomiting

6. If an officer's weekly salary is increased from $480 to $540, then the percent of increase is ______ percent. 6.____

   A. 10 B. 11 1/9 C. 12 1/2 D. 20

7. Suppose that one-half the officers in a department have served for more than ten years and one-third have served for more than 15 years. Then, the fraction of officers who have served between ten and fifteen years is 7.____

   A. 1/3 B. 1/5 C. 1/6 D. 1/12

8. In a city prison there are four floors on which prisoners are housed. The top floor houses one-quarter of the inmates, the bottom floor houses one-sixth of the inmates, one-third are housed on the second floor. The rest of the inmates are housed on the third floor. If there are 90 inmates housed on the third floor, the TOTAL number of inmates housed on all four floors together is 8.____

   A. 270 B. 360 C. 450 D. 540

9. Suppose that ten percent of those who commit serious crimes are convicted and that fifteen percent of those convicted are sentenced for more than 3 years. 9.____
The percentage of those committing serious crimes who are sentenced for more than 3 years is ______ percent.

A. 15 B. 1.5 C. .15 D. .015

10. Assume that there are 1,100 employees in a city agency. Of these, 15 percent are officers, 80 percent of whom are attorneys; of the attorneys, two-fifths have been with the agency over five years. 10.____
Then, the number of officers who are attorneys and have over five years experience with the agency is MOST NEARLY

A. 45 B. 53 C. 132 D. 165

11. An employee who has 500 cartons of supplies to pack can pack them at the rate of 50 an hour. After this employee has worked for 1/2 hour, he is joined by another employee who can pack 45 cartons an hour. 11.____
Assuming that both employees can maintain their respective rates of speed, then the TOTAL number of hours required to pack all the cartons is

A. 4 1/2 B. 5 C. 5 1/2 D. 6 1/2

12. Thirty-six officers can complete an assignment in 22 days. Assuming that all officers work at the same rate of speed, the number of officers that would be needed to complete this assignment in 12 days is 12.____

A. 42 B. 54 C. 66 D. 72

Questions 13-15.

DIRECTIONS: Questions 13 through 15 are to be answered on the basis of the table below. Data for certain categories have been omitted from the table. You are to calculate the missing numbers if needed to answer the questions.

	2007	2008	Numerical Increase
Correction Officers	1,226	1,347	
Court Officers		529	34
Deputy Sheriffs	38	40	
Supervisors			
	2,180	2,414	

13. The number in the *Supervisors* group in 2007 was MOST NEARLY 13.____

A. 500 B. 475 C. 450 D. 425

14. The LARGEST percentage increase from 2007 to 2008 was in the group of 14.____

A. Correction Officers B. Court Officers
C. Deputy Sheriffs D. Supervisors

15. In 2008, the ratio of the number of Correction Officers to the total of the other three categories of employees was MOST NEARLY 15.____

A. 1:1 B. 2:1 C. 3:1 D. 4:1

16. A directed verdict is made by a court when 16.____

A. the facts are not disputed
B. the defendant's motion for a directed verdict has been denied
C. there is no question of law involved
D. neither party has moved for a directed verdict

17. Papers on appeal of a criminal case do NOT include one of the following: 17.____

A. Summons
B. Minutes of trial
C. Complaint
D. Intermediate motion papers

18. A pleading titled *Smith vs. Jones, et al* indicates 18.____

A. two plaintiffs
B. two defendants
C. more than two defendants
D. unknown defendants

19. A District Attorney makes a *prima facie* case when 19.____

A. there is proof of guilt beyond a reasonable doubt
B. the evidence is sufficient to convict in the absence of rebutting evidence
C. the prosecution presents more evidence than the defense
D. the defendant fails to take the stand

20. A person is NOT qualified to act as a trial juror in a criminal action if he or she 20.____

A. has been convicted previously of a misdemeanor
B. is under 18 years of age
C. has scruples against the death penalty
D. does not own property of a value at least $500

21. A court clerk who falsifies a court record commits a(n) 21.____

A. misdemeanor
B. offense
C. felony
D. no crime, but automatically forfeits his tenure

22. Insolent and contemptuous behavior to a judge during a court of record proceeding is punishable as 22.____

A. civil contempt
B. criminal contempt
C. disorderly conduct
D. a disorderly person

23. Offering a bribe to a court clerk would not constitute a crime UNLESS the 23.____

A. court clerk accepted the bribe
B. bribe consisted of money
C. bribe was given with intent to influence the court clerk in his official functions
D. court was actually in session

24. A defendant comes to trial in the same court in which he had previously been defendant in a similar case. 24.____
The court officer should

A. tell him, *Knew we'd be seeing you again*
B. tell newspaper reporters what he knows of the previous action
C. treat him the same as he would any other defendant
D. warn the judge that the man had previously been a defendant

25. Suppose in conversation with you, an attorney strongly criticizes a ruling of the judge and you believe the attorney to be correct. 25.____
You should

A. assure him you feel the same way
B. tell him the judge knows the law
C. tell him to ask for an exception
D. refuse to discuss the matter

26. Assume that you are a court officer. A woman sees you in the hall and attempts to register a complaint that her husband raped her two hours earlier. 26.____
Which one of the following is the MOST appropriate action for you to take FIRST in this case?

A. Refer her to Family Court.
B. Advise her that her husband has not committed any crime.
C. Ask her for additional information about the circumstances surrounding her allegation so that you may refer her to the proper office or agency.
D. Have her sign a criminal information in the court.

27. Which one of the following is the BEST example of a privileged communication which is NOT admissible as evidence in a court of law without the consent of the communicator? 27.____

A. Client to his accountant
B. Informant to a law enforcement officer
C. Parent to his child
D. Defendant to his spouse

28. A court officer has many contacts with the public. In these contacts, it is MOST important that he 28.____

A. be brief and complete in his answers
B. be courteous and helpful
C. go along with what they ask
D. know the law

29. Suppose a witness becomes engaged in a very heated argument with an attorney who is cross-examining him. The court officer should 29.____

A. ask the attorney to avoid exciting the witness
B. ask the judge if he wishes any action to be taken
C. await the judge's order before interceding
D. caution the witness to be more respectful

30. Suppose that you are a court officer stationed at the door of the courtroom to prevent anyone from entering while the judge is charging the jury. A man whom you recognize as a City Councilman, accompanied by a woman, attempts to enter the courtroom. The BEST action for you to take is to 30.____

A. apologize and explain why they cannot be permitted to enter
B. permit the man to enter since he is a Councilman but exclude the woman
C. permit them to enter since the judge would surely make an exception for them
D. send a note in to the judge to find if they may be permitted to enter

31. It is desirable that a court officer acquire a knowledge of the procedures of the court to which he is assigned MAINLY because such knowledge will help him 31.____

A. become familiar with anti-social behavior
B. discharge his duties properly
C. gain insight into causes of crime
D. in any personal legal proceeding

32. Since he is a city employee, a court officer who refuses to waive immunity from prosecution when called on to testify in court automatically terminates his employment. From this statement ONLY, it may be BEST inferred that 32.____

A. a court officer is a city employee
B. all city employees are court officers
C. city employees may be fired only for malfeasance
D. court attendants who waive immunity may not be prosecuted

33. Referees of the Civil Court are former judges of this court who have served at least ten years and whose term of office terminated at the age of 55 or over, or any judge who has served in a court of record and has retired. According to this statement, a person can be a referee of the Civil Court ONLY if he 33.____

A. has been a judge
B. has retired
C. has served at least 10 years in the court
D. meets certain age requirements

34. Assume that you are assigned to a jury room where you are to guard the jury until 4 P.M. Your relief does not arrive and the jury is still deliberating. Of the following, the BEST action for you to take is to 34.____

A. ask the foreman of the jury to assume responsibility until your relief arrives
B. find out what the jurors may need, get it, and then lock them in for the night
C. inform your supervisor but remain on duty until you are relieved
D. wait until 5 P.M., your usual closing time, and then leave if the relief has not arrived by then

35. When, at a trial, a piece of evidence is tagged as *Exhibit A,* the CHIEF purpose is to 35.____

A. assure its return to the owner
B. make it possible to examine it for fingerprints without chance of error
C. make it possible to identify and refer to it easily
D. prevent the defendant from denying he had it

36. In one case, a mistrial was declared because the indictment used the pronoun he instead of she. 36.____
The MOST useful information a court attendant can derive from this statement is that

A. accuracy is important
B. mistrial is a legal term
C. one must always use good grammar
D. to misrepresent is criminal

37. Suppose a newspaper reporter asks you for information about what happened at a trial where the judge had ordered the courtroom cleared of reporters and spectators. 37.____
You should

A. give him the information he wants
B. refer him to the judge for information
C. refuse to talk to him unless reporters from other papers are present
D. give him misleading information

38. Assume that you are the court officer on duty outside the judge's chambers in the court house. One day, one of the judges informs you that he will be too busy that day to see any visitors, and he tells you to refer them to his secretary for new appointments. Later in the day, an important visitor comes in and asks to see the judge about urgent business. 38.____
Of the following, the BEST course of action for you to take in this situation is to

A. ask the visitor to come back another day when the judge may be able to see him
B. call the judge on the phone and tell him that the visitor has urgent business to discuss with him
C. refer the visitor to one of the other judges who may be present in chambers
D. tell the visitor that the judge is not available, but his secretary may be able to help him or make a new appointment

39. To gain a verdict against X in a trial, it was necessary to show that he could have been at Y Street at 5 P.M. 39.____
It was proven that he was seen at Z Street at 4:45 P.M. The question that MUST be answered to show whether the verdict should be against X is:

A. How long does it take to get from Z Street to Y Street?
B. In what sort of neighborhood is Y Street located?
C. Was X acting suspiciously on the day in question?
D. Who was with X when he was seen at Z Street at 4:45 P.M.?

40. If, at the instructions of the judge, a court officer calls the name of a defendant in a lawsuit and the person does not answer, the court officer should FIRST 40.____

A. ask the judge if he called the person's name correctly
B. call the person's name again
C. look outside the doors of the courtroom for the defendant
D. tell the judge the person doesn't answer

41. When X is accused of having cheated Y of a sum of money and Y is proven to have been deprived of the money, there is an additional requirement for a verdict against X. 41.____
The additional requirement is to prove that

A. the money was stolen from Y
B. X had the money after Y had it
C. X had the money before Y had it
D. X cheated Y of the money

42. Assume that you are on duty in a courtroom and during the judge's absence one of the witnesses for a pending case becomes very angry about the delay. 42.____
Of the following, the BEST action for you to take is to

A. listen to him until he calms down and then explain the reason for the delay
B. tell him your court is no different from any other court
C. walk away from him so that you will not get involved in a dispute
D. warn him that the judge may be back at any minute and will hold him in contempt

43. Assume that you are assigned to the post outside judge's chambers in the court house. A visitor tells you he has an appointment with Judge Jones who is expected to arrive shortly. He asks for permission to wait in the judge's office which is unoccupied at the present time. 43.____
For you to permit him to wait there would be

A. *wise;* the judge would no doubt wish to speak to the man privately
B. *wise;* it would keep the anteroom where you are stationed clear, allowing other employees to work without any disturbance
C. *unwise;* it is rude to allow a visitor to sit alone in an office
D. *unwise;* there may be confidential material on the judge's desk or bookcases

44. A court officer shall not receive a gift from any defendant or other person on the defendant's behalf. 44.____
The BEST explanation for this rule is that

A. acceptance of a gift has no significance
B. defendants cannot usually afford gifts
C. favors may be expected in return
D. gifts are only an expression of good will

45. When a jury is selected, the attorney for each side has a right to refuse to accept a certain number of prospective jurors without giving any reason therefor. 45.____
The reason for this is MAINLY that

A. attorneys can exclude persons likely to be biased even though no prejudice is admitted
B. persons who will suffer economically by being summoned for jury duty can be excused forthwith
C. relatives of the litigants can be excused thus insuring a fair trial for each side
D. there will be a greater number of people from which the jury can be selected

46. Where the defendant in a criminal case is too poor to afford counsel, the court will assign one and he will be paid by the government. 46.____
The principle BEST established by this statement is that

A. it is improper for the government to provide both prosecuting and defending counsel in a trial
B. laws are usually violated because of poverty and defendants are too poor to employ counsel
C. only wealthy law violators may hope to be represented by competent counsel
D. the government is obligated to shield the innocent as well as punish the guilty

47. If a visitor to the court asks foolish questions, the BEST action for the court officer to take is to 47.____

    A. answer in a brusque manner to discourage further foolish questions
    B. refer the questioner to his supervisor
    C. answer them the same way as he would any other questions
    D. ignore them since the person doesn't really expect an answer

48. A man plus a uniform makes a good court officer. This statement is FALSE because 48.____

    A. a court officer is also required to wear a badge
    B. a good court officer is not made merely by putting on a uniform
    C. it makes no mention of the fact that the uniform must be neat
    D. patrolmen as well as court officers wear uniforms

49. It is a frequent misconception that court officers can be recruited from those registers established for the recruitment of city police or firemen. While it is true that many common qualifications are found in all of these, specific standards for court work are indicated, varying with the size, geographical location, and policies of the court. 49.____
    According to this paragraph ONLY, it may BEST be inferred that

    A. a successful court officer must have some qualifications not required of a policeman or fireman
    B. qualifications which make a successful patrolman will also make a successful fireman
    C. the same qualifications are required of a court officer regardless of the court to which he is assigned
    D. the successful court officer is required to be both more intelligent and stronger than a fireman

50. One of the duties of a court officer is to assist the public with their problems. 50.____
    A PROPER exercise of this duty by a court officer would be for the officer to

    A. advise members of the public to settle their differences out of court
    B. advise a member of the public how to fill out forms required by the court
    C. lend money to a member of the public to pay the required court fees
    D. recommend a lawyer to a member of the public who does not have one

KEY (CORRECT ANSWERS)

1. A	11. C	21. C	31. B	41. D
2. C	12. C	22. B	32. A	42. A
3. D	13. D	23. C	33. A	43. D
4. C	14. D	24. C	34. C	44. C
5. A	15. A	25. D	35. C	45. A
6. C	16. A	26. C	36. A	46. D
7. C	17. D	27. D	37. B	47. C
8. B	18. C	28. B	38. D	48. B
9. B	19. B	29. C	39. A	49. A
10. B	20. B	30. A	40. B	50. B

EXAMINATION SECTION
TEST 1

DIRECTIONS: Each question or incomplete statement is followed by several suggested answers or completions. Select the one that BEST answers the question or completes the statement. *PRINT THE LETTER OF THE CORRECT ANSWER IN THE SPACE AT THE RIGHT.*

1. Which of the following is the LEAST important factor to consider in surveying the physical layout of a building for traffic flow? 1.____

   A. Location of windows
   B. Number of entrances
   C. Number of exits
   D. Location of first aid rooms

2. The major purpose of any security program in a large organization is to prevent unlawful acts. 2.____
   If adequate patrol coverage is provided at a given location, it is MOST likely that

   A. crimes will not be committed
   B. undesirables will not enter the building
   C. unlawful acts will increase in the long run
   D. there will be less opportunity to commit a crime

3. The MOST frequent cause of fires in public facilities is 3.____

   A. incinerators
   B. vandalism
   C. electrical sources
   D. smoking on the job

4. After bomb threats are received, it is sometimes necessary to evacuate a facility. How long BEFORE the threatened time of explosion should a facility be evacuated? 4.____
   At least _______ minutes.

   A. 15
   B. 25
   C. 50
   D. 60

5. Once a facility is evacuated because of a bomb threat, how much time should pass before the public and employees are allowed to enter the building? 5.____
   _______ minutes.

   A. 10
   B. 20
   C. 40
   D. 60

6. Of the following locations in public buildings, the one which is the LEAST likely place for bombs to be planted is in 6.____

   A. storerooms
   B. bathrooms
   C. cafeterias
   D. waste receptacles

7. The one of the following that is the surest means of establishing positive identification of someone entering a facility is by 7.____

   A. personal recognition
   B. I.D. badge
   C. social security card
   D. driver's license

8. The one of the following which most probably would NOT be included in a police record report concerning an incident at a facility is the 8.____

A. name of complainant or injured party
B. name of the investigating officer
C. statement of each witness
D. religion of complainant or injured party

9. Preventing trouble is one of the primary concerns of special officers. 9.____
When dealing with unruly groups of people who threaten to become violent, which of the following is a measure which should NOT be taken?

A. Maintain close surveillance of such groups
B. Try to contact the leaders of the group regardless of their militancy
C. Keep the officer force alerted
D. Have the officer force deal aggressively with provocations

10. Of the following, the MOST important factor to consider in the deployment of officers dealing with a client population is the officers' ability to 10.____

A. remain calm
B. look stern
C. evaluate personality
D. take a firm stand

11. Assume that an offender is struggling with a group of officers who are trying to arrest him. 11.____
What force, if any, can be used to overcome this resistance?

A. The amount of force acceptable to the public
B. The amount of force necessary to restrain the offender and protect the officers
C. Any amount of force that is acceptable to the officers at the scene
D. No force may be used until the police arrive

12. Assume that a fire is discovered at your work location. The one of the following actions which would be INAPPROPRIATE for you to take is to 12.____

A. notify the telephone operator
B. station a reliable person at the entrance
C. open all windows and doors in the area
D. start evacuating the area

13. If a person has an object caught in his throat or air passage but is breathing adequately, which one of the following should you do? 13.____

A. Probe for the object
B. Force him to drink water
C. Lay him over your arm and slap him between the shoulder blades
D. Allow him to cough and to assume the position he finds most comfortable

14. The one of the following methods which should NOT be used to report a fire is to 14.____

A. call 911
B. pull the handle in the red box on the street corner
C. call the fire department county numbers listed in each county directory
D. call 411

15. Assume that an officer, alone in a building at night, smells the strong odor of cooking or heating gas. In addition to airing the building and making sure that he is not overcome, it would be BEST for the officer to call 15.____

A. his superior at his home and ask for instructions
B. for a plumber from the department of public works
C. 911 for police and fire help
D. the emergency number at Con Edison

16. Of the following situations, the one that is MOST dangerous for an officer is when he 16.____

A. investigates suspicious persons and circumstances
B. finds a burglary in progress or pursues burglary suspects
C. attempts an arrest or finds a robbery in progress
D. patrols on the overnight shift

17. An officer on security patrol generally should spend MOST of his time 17.____

A. checking doors and locks
B. helping the public and answering questions
C. chasing criminals and looking for clues
D. writing reports on unusual incidents

18. The one of the following that is an ACCEPTABLE way to arrest a person is to 18.____

A. tell him to report to the nearest police precinct
B. send a summons to his permanent address
C. tell him in person that he is under arrest
D. show him handcuffs and ask him to come along

19. A carbon dioxide fire extinguisher is BEST suited for extinguishing ______ fires. 19.____

A. paper B. rag C. rubbish D. grease

20. A pressurized water or soda-acid fire extinguisher is BEST suited for extinguishing ______ fires. 20.____

A. wood B. gasoline
C. electrical D. magnesium

21. The one of the following statements that does NOT apply to the use of handcuffs is that they 21.____

A. are used as temporary restraining devices
B. eliminate the need for vigilance
C. cannot be opened without keys
D. are used to secure a violent person

22. The one of the following that is GENERALLY a crime against the person is 22.____

A. trespass B. burglary C. robbery D. arson

23. Of the following, the SAFEST way of escape from an office in a burning building is generally the 23.____

A. stairway
B. rooftop
C. passenger elevator
D. freight elevator

24. In attempting to control a possible riot situation, an officer pushed his way into a crowd gathered outside the building and tried to cause confusion by arguing with members of the group. 24.____
This procedure NORMALLY is considered

A. *desirable;* any violence that occurs will remain outside the building
B. *desirable;* the crowd will break into smaller groups and disperse
C. *undesirable;* to maintain control of the situation, the officer must not become part of the crowd
D. *undesirable;* the supervisor should stay clear of the scene

25. Which one of the following is MOST effective in making officers more safety-minded? 25.____

A. Maintaining an up-to-date library of the latest safety literature
B. Reading daily safety bulletins at roll-call
C. Holding informal group safety meetings periodically
D. Offering prizes for good safety slogans and displays

KEY (CORRECT ANSWERS)

1.	A	11.	B
2.	D	12.	C
3.	C	13.	D
4.	A	14.	D
5.	D	15.	D
6.	C	16.	C
7.	A	17.	A
8.	D	18.	C
9.	D	19.	D
10.	A	20.	A

21. B
22. C
23. A
24. C
25. C

TEST 2

DIRECTIONS: Each question or incomplete statement is followed by several suggested answers or completions. Select the one that BEST answers the question or completes the statement. *PRINT THE LETTER OF THE CORRECT ANSWER IN THE SPACE AT THE RIGHT.*

1. Assume that an angry crowd of some 75 to 100 people has built up in one of the hallways of a center and that only one superior officer and two subordinate officers are on duty in the building. A glass panel in one of the stairway doors has just been broken under the pressure of the crowd and a bench has been hurled down a flight of stairs. The one of the following actions that the superior officer SHOULD take in this situation is to 1.____

   A. push his way into the crowd and try to reason with them
   B. order the two other officers to try to quiet the crowd
   C. call the police on 911 and meet them outside the building
   D. do nothing at this point in order to avoid a riot

2. One of the duties and responsibilities of a supervisor is to test the knowledge of the officers concerning their post conditions. 2.____
   This should be done if the officer's assignment is

   A. fixed only
   B. roving only
   C. roving only in a troublesome spot
   D. either fixed or roving

3. An officer discovers early one morning that an office in the building he guards has been burglarized. 3.____
   Of the following, it is important for the officer to FIRST

   A. go through the building and look for suspects
   B. call the police and protect the area and whatever evidence exists until they arrive
   C. allow people into their offices as they come to work
   D. examine, sort, and handle all evidence before the police get there

4. Assume that two officers are interrogating one suspect. How should these officers position themselves during the interrogation? 4.____

   A. One officer should stand on either side of the suspect.
   B. One officer should stand to the right of the suspect, and the other officer should stand behind the suspect.
   C. Both officers should stand to the right of the suspect.
   D. One officer should stand to the right of the suspect, and the other officer should stand in front of the suspect.

5. A witness who takes an oath to testify truly and who states as true any matter which he knows to be false is guilty of 5.____

   A. perjury B. libel C. slander D. fraud

6. An officer checking a substance suspected of containing narcotics should GENERALLY 6.____

   A. taste it in small amounts
   B. send it to a laboratory for analysis
   C. smell it for its distinctive odor
   D. examine it for its unusual texture

7. A certain center is situated in an area where frequent outbreaks of hostilities seem to be focused on the center itself. 7.____
   Which of the following BEST explains why the center may be a target for hostile acts? It

   A. serves community needs
   B. represents governmental authority
   C. represents all ethnic groups
   D. serves as a neutral battlefield

8. An officer often deals with people who might be addicted to drugs. 8.____
   The one of the following symptoms which is NOT generally an indication of drug addiction is

   A. dilation of the eye pupils
   B. frequent yawning and sneezing
   C. a deep, rasping cough
   D. continual itching of the arms and legs

9. In emergency situations, panic will MOST probably occur when people are 9.____

   A. unexpectedly confronted with a terrorizing condition from which there appears to be no escape
   B. angry and violent
   C. anxious about circumstances which are not obvious, easily visible or within the immediate area
   D. familiar with the effects of the emergency

10. The one of the following actions on the part of a person that would NOT be considered *resisting arrest* is 10.____

    A. retreating and running away
    B. saying, *You can't arrest me*
    C. pushing the officer aside
    D. pulling away from an officer's grasp

11. Which of the following items would NOT be considered an APPROPRIATE item of uniform for an officer to wear while on duty? 11.____

    A. Reefer type overcoat
    B. Leather laced shoes with flat soles
    C. White socks
    D. Cap cover with cap device displayed

12. What can happen to an officer if the leather thong on his night stick is NOT twisted correctly? 12.____
The

A. baton may be taken out of the officer's hand
B. officer's wrist may be broken
C. leather will tear more easily
D. officer's arm may be injured

13. The one of the following kinds of information which SHOULD be included in the log book is 13.____

A. any important matter of police information
B. an item noted in Standard Operating Procedures only
C. everything of general interest
D. a crime or offense only

14. While on patrol at your work location, you receive a call that an assault has taken place. Upon your arrival at the scene, the victim, who has severe lacerations, informs you that the assailant ran into a nearby basement. 14.____
After apprehending the suspect, the type of search you should conduct is a ______ search.

A. wall B. frisk C. body D. strip

15. A tactical force is valuable in MOST emergency situations PRIMARILY because of its 15.____

A. location
B. morale
C. flexibility
D. size

16. An officer should be encouraged to talk easily and frankly when he is dealing with his superior. 16.____
In order to encourage such free communication, it would be MOST appropriate for a superior to behave in a(n)

A. *sincere* manner; assure the officer that you will deal with him honestly and openly
B. *official* manner; you are a superior officer and must always act formally with subordinates
C. *investigative* manner; you must probe and question to get to a basis of trust
D. *unemotional* manner; the officer's emotions and background should play no part in your dealings with him

17. Research findings show that an increase in free communication within an agency GENERALLY results in which one of the following? 17.____

A. Improved morale and productivity
B. Increased promotional opportunities
C. An increase in authority
D. A spirit of honesty

18. Assume that you are a superior officer and your superiors have given you a new arrest procedure to be followed. Before passing this information on to your subordinates, the one of the following actions that you should take FIRST is to 18.____

   A. ask your superiors to send out a memorandum to the entire staff
   B. clarify the procedure in your own mind
   C. set up a training course to provide instructions on the new procedure
   D. write a memorandum to your subordinates

19. Communication is necessary for an organization to be effective. 19.____
The one of the following which is LEAST important for most communication systems is that

   A. messages are sent quickly and directly to the person who needs them to operate
   B. information should be conveyed understandably and accurately
   C. the method used to transmit information should be kept secret so that security can be maintained
   D. senders of messages must know how their messages were received and acted upon

20. Which one of the following is the CHIEF advantage of listening willingly to subordinate officers and encouraging them to talk freely and honestly? 20.____
It

   A. reveals to superiors the degree to which ideas that are passed down are accepted by subordinates
   B. reduces the participation of subordinates in the operation of the department
   C. encourages officers to try for promotion
   D. enables officers to learn about security leaks on the part of officials

21. A superior may be informed through either oral or written reports. 21.____
Which one of the following is an ADVANTAGE of using oral reports?

   A. There is no need for a formal record of the report.
   B. An exact duplicate of the report is not easily transmitted to others.
   C. A good oral report requires little time for preparation.
   D. An oral report involves two-way communication between a subordinate and his superior.

22. Of the following, the MOST important reason why officers should communicate effectively with the public is to 22.____

   A. improve the public's understanding of information that is important for them to know
   B. establish a friendly relationship
   C. obtain information about the kinds of people who come to the center
   D. convince the public that services are adequate

23. Officers should generally NOT use phrases like *too hard, too easy,* and *a lot* principally because such phrases 23.____

   A. may be offensive to some minority groups
   B. are too informal

C. mean different things to different people
D. are difficult to remember

24. The ability to communicate clearly and concisely is an important element in effective leadership. Which of the following statements about oral and written communication is GENERALLY true? 24.____

A. Oral communication is more time-consuming.
B. Written communication is more likely to be misinterpreted.
C. Oral communication is useful only in emergencies.
D. Written communication is useful mainly when giving information to fewer than twenty people.

25. Rumors can often have harmful and disruptive effects on an organization. Which one of the following is the BEST way to prevent rumors from becoming a problem? 25.____

A. Refuse to act on rumors, thereby making them less believable
B. Increase the amount of information passed along by the *grapevine*
C. Distribute as much factual information as possible
D. Provide training in report writing

KEY (CORRECT ANSWERS)

1.	C	11.	C
2.	D	12.	A
3.	B	13.	A
4.	B	14.	A
5.	A	15.	C
6.	B	16.	A
7.	B	17.	A
8.	C	18.	B
9.	A	19.	C
10.	B	20.	A

21. D
22. A
23. C
24. B
25. C

EXAMINATION SECTION
TEST 1

DIRECTIONS: Each question or incomplete statement is followed by several suggested answers or completions. Select the one that BEST answers the question or completes the statement. *PRINT THE LETTER OF THE CORRECT ANSWER IN THE SPACE AT THE RIGHT.*

1. As a superior officer, you have the responsibility of deciding whether some of your duties should be delegated to subordinate officers. 1.____
The delegation of certain duties to subordinates is GENERALLY considered

   A. *inadvisable;* subordinates should not share your responsibilities
   B. *advisable;* this will help to prevent you from getting bogged down with minor details and problems
   C. *inadvisable;* you can probably do all parts of your job better than anyone else can
   D. *advisable;* more time can therefore be devoted to day-to-day operations and less to long-range planning

2. Assume that you are a superior officer and that one of your subordinates is careless in the performance of his job. 2.____
Of the following, it would be MOST important for you, when helping this employee, to realize that

   A. punitive methods produce better long-term results than non-punitive methods
   B. most problem officers require strict supervision rather than counseling and training
   C. the superior can often play a large part in changing employee patterns of work
   D. if orders are given in detail, carelessness will be eliminated

3. One of the key qualities of a good superior officer is his ability to balance his work load against the time available to him to complete the job. 3.____
Of the following, the BEST procedure for a superior to follow in establishing his work priorities is to

   A. organize tasks according to urgency without regard to importance
   B. undertake all important, difficult tasks in any order and delegate the routine work to subordinates
   C. assign all work to various subordinates and guide their handling of the problems
   D. delegate those problems that can be solved by others and personally handle the difficult, most pressing issues first

4. It is generally CORRECT to state that the planning process within an organization 4.____

   A. is a management responsibility and should not involve the participation of operating personnel
   B. should include long-range programs and goals, and should not include activities which can be carried out within a few weeks or months
   C. is to be used in order to develop and improve practices and procedures but is not to be used in applying these procedures in actual operations
   D. should be used at all supervisory levels since each superior officer must determine how to accomplish tasks and what resources are needed

5. Assume you are a superior officer and one of your subordinates, who has a low performance rating, has made a good suggestion that will make his job easier.
The BEST course of action for you to take in this situation is to 5.____

A. disregard his suggestion, since he is only trying to do as little work as possible
B. use his suggestion, since it is a positive suggestion and could motivate him to do better work
C. use his suggestion, but transfer him to a position where he will not benefit from it
D. disregard his suggestion, and have a talk with him about his poor performance

6. The use of different criteria to rate employees in different jobs is GENERALLY considered 6.____

A. *desirable,* chiefly because people should be treated as individuals with varying strengths and weaknesses
B. *undesirable,* chiefly because the use of different criteria results in unfair evaluations
C. *desirable,* chiefly because people in different jobs cannot always be rated on the basis of the same criteria
D. *undesirable,* chiefly because ratings that are standardized cannot be compared

7. In preparing an annual division budget for equipment and supplies, the one of the following methods that is MOST appropriate to use is to 7.____

A. combine the previous year's division budget with the estimate of any additional or reduced needs for the coming year
B. determine what amount the department will approve and use that figure
C. overestimate division needs by 10% because the department will automatically reduce the figure that is first submitted
D. underestimate division needs because a reduction in the budget indicates increased efficiency

8. All of the following are objectives of in-service training EXCEPT 8.____

A. discovering and developing skills
B. providing better service to the public
C. raising the status of the service
D. eliminating the need for performance evaluations

9. From a management point of view, the one of the following that is the MOST important advantage of regular personnel performance appraisals is that they 9.____

A. help an officer to prepare for promotion examinations
B. pinpoint an officer's personality weaknesses
C. provide an opportunity for regular discussions, including counseling, between an officer and his superior
D. provide the setting to explain the reasons for disciplinary actions which an officer might not understand

10. Assume that an officer arrests a man for assaulting a woman in the building he is guarding. Later, while the suspect is being searched, the officer finds a switchblade knife, four bags of heroin, and three hypodermic syringes in his clothing.
In these circumstances, the possession of which of the following items might indicate a violation of some law? 10.____

A. Only the heroin
B. The heroin, the hypodermic syringes, but not the switchblade knife
C. The switchblade knife, the heroin, but not the hypodermic syringes
D. The switchblade knife, the heroin, and the hypodermic syringes

11. Upon arriving at the scene of a serious crime, a superior officer SHOULD instruct his subordinates to 11.____

A. protect the crime scene
B. collect, mark, and evaluate evidence
C. brief the news media on the status of the crime
D. prevent medical personnel from entering the crime scene

12. In standard police terminology, the term *fugitive warrant* refers to 12.____

A. any type of warrant that is not a local warrant
B. a written request for the detention of a suspect
C. a warrant for a person who leaves his local jurisdiction and commits an offense in another jurisdiction
D. a type of booking made when a person wanted by an out-of-state jurisdiction is arrested by local officers

13. The one of the following actions with respect to an offender that an officer should NOT take when an infraction has been committed is to 13.____

A. inform the offender of his rights
B. punish the offender
C. warn the offender of possible consequences
D. apprehend the offender using appropriate force

14. Perimeter barriers, intrusion devices, protective lighting, and a personnel identification system are used for good physical security of a building.
An objective of personnel identification and control is to 14.____

A. exempt authorized personnel from compliance with annoying entry and departure procedures
B. detect unauthorized persons who attempt to gain entry
C. eliminate the need for expensive perimeter barriers and intrusion alarms
D. allow an increased number of gates and perimeter entrances to be operated at the same time during peak activity hours

15. A true copy of the testimony taken in a criminal action is known as a(n) 15.____

A. verdict
B. transcript
C. judgment
D. indictment

16. The process of gathering information during an investigation usually involves interviewing or interrogating witnesses. 16.____
Interviews or interrogations are *primarily* used for all of the following purposes EXCEPT to

A. establish the facts of a possible crime to provide the investigator with leads
B. verify information already known to the police
C. secure evidence that may establish the guilt or complicity of a suspect
D. prevent the person questioned from giving an account of the incident under investigation to newspapers

17. Of the following, the BEST reason to apprehend a narcotics violator out of view of the public is to 17.____

A. prevent the drug user from becoming violent
B. allow the suspect to *save face* with his friends
C. prevent the knowledge of his apprehension from reaching any collaborators
D. keep the suspect from disposing of evidence

18. Assume that you, a superior officer, are planning the physical security operation at a facility. One of the problems you are faced with is that of casual thievery by staff. 18.____
Of the following, the BEST means of discouraging such thievery is by establishing

A. an aggressive security education program
B. adequate inventory control measures
C. spot search procedures
D. an effective key control system

19. Under an officer's scope of authority, all of the following actions would be proper EXCEPT 19.____

A. apprehending persons attempting to gain unauthorized access to any work location
B. enforcing the traffic control rules applicable to the work location
C. removing persons suspected of theft with a warning to them not to return
D. responding to protective alarm signals and other warning devices

20. One of the ways of deploying an officer force at the scene of a demonstration is called *strength in reserve.* This procedure involves having only a few officers police the demonstration while most are being held in reserve. Which one of the following is a DISADVANTAGE of this type of deployment? 20.____
It

A. permits the demonstrators to estimate the number of officers available
B. might result in a delay between a violent outbreak and the arrival of enough officers to handle the situation
C. prevents the superior officer from deploying his forces
D. does not permit rotation of the officers confronting the demonstrators

21. Of the following, the MOST important principle to keep in mind when making arrests is that 21.____

A. the absence of force will discourage resistance on the part of the offender
B. the arresting officer should assume, for his own safety, that the person to be arrested is dangerous
C. once the offender is arrested he should be kept at the scene of the arrest and questioned
D. in order to prevent violence, it is better to have too few officers making arrests than too many

22. Of the following steps, the one that an officer should take FIRST upon discovering a broken electrical power line while on duty is to 22.____

A. notify his supervisor
B. notify the electrical company
C. determine whether it is a live wire
D. take measures to protect and barricade the area

23. Assume you are a superior officer interrogating a suspect.
The FIRST question you ask him should usually pertain to 23.____

A. his name and address
B. a package which he may be carrying
C. where he has been
D. where he is going

24. Which one of the following statements concerning the interrogation of a juvenile is INCORRECT? 24.____

A. The juvenile should be advised of his rights.
B. The juvenile should be told as little as possible about the case.
C. A bond of mutual interest should be established with the juvenile.
D. The juvenile should be encouraged to ask the interrogator questions.

25. Assume that an intoxicated man has wandered into a center and is begging for money and harassing clients. Of the following, the MOST effective action to take in this situation would be to 25.____

A. call immediately for police assistance
B. take the man aside quietly and try to persuade him to move along
C. ask two or three male clients to help you take the man outside
D. arrest the man at once so that drunks will know they should stay away

KEY (CORRECT ANSWERS)

1. B
2. C
3. D
4. D
5. B

6. C
7. A
8. D
9. C
10. D

11. A
12. D
13. B
14. B
15. B

16. D
17. C
18. C
19. C
20. B

21. B
22. D
23. A
24. D
25. B

TEST 2

DIRECTIONS: Each question or incomplete statement is followed by several suggested answers or completions. Select the one that BEST answers the question or completes the statement. *PRINT THE LETTER OF THE CORRECT ANSWER IN THE SPACE AT THE RIGHT.*

1. Assume that you, a superior officer, have received a communication from one of your subordinates that his center has just received a *ticking* package. 1.____
   Of the following steps, the one that he should take FIRST is to

   A. notify the Police Department
   B. remove the package and soak it in water
   C. check the contents of the package
   D. evacuate the area

2. Assume that an individual suspected of drug abuse is apprehended. The suspect produces a prescription which he claims is for the drug found on his person. 2.____
   Which of the following actions should be taken NEXT?

   A. The prescription should be disregarded and the suspect should be arrested.
   B. Release the individual, but confiscate the drug in order to have a laboratory check its composition.
   C. The opinion of a medical doctor should be obtained.
   D. The suspect should be released since he has a prescription.

3. A mob has been defined as a group of individuals who commit lawless acts under the stimulus of intense excitement or agitation. 3.____
   All of the following are generally considered characteristics of a mob EXCEPT

   A. some degree of organization
   B. one or more leaders
   C. a common motive for action
   D. unemotional behavior

4. Which of the following would be IMPROPER for an officer to do while apprehending a suspect? 4.____

   A. Maintain a quiet voice and manner
   B. Remove the person from the scene as soon as possible in order to avoid conflict with the suspect and bystanders
   C. Allow the suspect to realize that the officer does not like persons who commit crimes
   D. Direct and accompany the person to an appropriate location

5. Which of the following is MOST appropriate for an officer to do while testifying as a witness in court? 5.____

   A. State the facts only of your own knowledge
   B. Argue with the defense attorney in order to show that your actions were proper
   C. Deny that you have discussed the case outside of court even if you have done so only with close friends
   D. Use as much technical language as possible in order to impress the jury with your knowledge

6. It is sometimes inadvisable to arrest the leaders of an unlawful demonstration immediately. 6.____
Of the following, the BEST reason to delay arresting the leaders of a demonstration is to

   A. permit them to restrain their followers who might threaten violence
   B. avoid unfavorable coverage by the press
   C. determine whether there is more than one charge involved
   D. let them get deeper in trouble so they will receive longer sentences when convicted

7. The one of the following approaches which would BEST foster good human relations when dealing with the public is for an officer to 7.____

   A. act very self-assured, thus gaining respect
   B. learn how to appeal to the biases and prejudices of others
   C. treat everyone in exactly the same way since everyone has the same needs
   D. appeal to the positive interests of others

8. The causes of many job complaints come not just from wages and working conditions but also from contacts with people on and off the job and from the officer's background and outlook on life. 8.____
Because of this, the BEST of the following ways for a superior officer to handle a complaint from a subordinate is generally to

   A. talk to the officer for the purpose of getting him to withdraw his complaint
   B. get as much information as possible to try to determine the real causes of the complaint
   C. postpone action on the complaint since conditions change so rapidly that it is useless to try to act quickly on a complaint
   D. handle each complaint as quickly as possible without looking into the motives for the complaint

9. In every unit certain officers are more cooperative than others. 9.____
The one of the following that is MOST likely to occur with regard to supervising such cooperative officers is that they

   A. are more easily intimidated
   B. are often assigned to difficult jobs
   C. are unfriendly to the general public
   D. assume a supervisor's position in dealing with others

10. Assume that you are a superior officer and that one of your subordinate officers comes to you with a complaint about an officer under his command. After listening to a few of the details, you suspect that his complaint is not justified. 10.____
Considering this, you should do all of the following during this initial conversation EXCEPT

   A. listen with interest until the subordinate officer finishes making his complaint
   B. tell the subordinate officer that you will investigate the matter further
   C. inform the subordinate that his complaint is invalid
   D. ask the subordinate officer further questions about his complaint

11. As a superior officer, you may receive complaints about the department or individual officers from the public. 11.____
Of the following, the PROPER attitude to take with regard to such complaints is that they

A. are often helpful in determining how to give the public better service
B. cause poor morale in the service and should not be revealed to subordinates
C. are useful as a basis for disciplining officers who have been troublesome in the past
D. take up too much of an officer's time and should not be accepted

12. One of the people present at a local parent-teacher organization meeting complained about the time it took for him to be taken care of at an agency office. A superior officer, present at the meeting, stood up and explained to the person and the group that there was no personal discrimination involved because the normal procedures took a while and that everyone spent about the same amount of time in the office. 12.____
In this situation, the action of the superior officer was

A. *proper,* mainly because it will show the group how much he knows about agency operations
B. *improper,* mainly because he should tell the man who complained to check first with the agency before complaining
C. *proper,* mainly because he helped to clear up a misunderstanding
D. *improper,* mainly because the officer should not discuss his agency in public

13. Assume that you are a superior officer and that you have begun a campaign to encourage your subordinates to be prompt in reporting for work. One of your subordinates requests that he be allowed to arrive a half hour late in the morning while his wife is in the hospital as a maternity patient. 13.____
Of the following actions, it would be BEST in this situation for you to

A. *refuse* the request, claiming it would be unfair to others to make an exception
B. *grant* the request, telling your other subordinates the reason for this exception
C. *refuse* the request, blaming the central office for having inflexible rules
D. *grant* the request, making it clear to all that this will be the last exception

14. Authorities agree that keeping rumors to a minimum is one of the goals of communication. 14.____
Which of the following is NOT consistent with this goal?

A. Distribute information that will tend to make rumors unnecessary
B. Reduce the social distance between top management and the lower supervisors
C. Stress the development of downward rather than upward channels of communication
D. Understand the emotional elements that cause stress

15. Of the following, the MOST important factor in determining the success or failure of communication between officers and the public is the 15.____

A. attitude of the public toward the officers prior to and during the communication
B. use of proper channels of communication within the organization
C. use of the mass media to change the public's attitude from negative to positive
D. increase in opportunities for personal contact between the officers and the public

16. Assume that you are a superior officer concerned with the effective use of praise and criticism to motivate your subordinates. 16.____
Of the following statements, the one that is EQUALLY TRUE of praise and criticism is that both should generally be

A. directed mainly toward the act instead of the person
B. given often and with no restrictions
C. given in public for the greatest effect
D. directed toward group efforts rather than individual efforts

17. Which of the following actions on the part of a superior officer is MOST likely to improve upward communication between his subordinates and himself? 17.____

A. Delay acting on undesirable working conditions until complaints from subordinates have reached top management
B. Make the time to listen to subordinates' ideas
C. Resist becoming involved with the personal problems of subordinates
D. Discourage communications that indicate which policies may have resulted in poor performance

18. Assume that you are a recently appointed superior officer and are told that one of your subordinates is a chronic complainer. 18.____
In this situation, which of the following steps should you take FIRST?

A. Report your subordinate to higher authority
B. Discipline your subordinate for his poor performance
C. Change your subordinate's tour of duty
D. Ask your subordinate for a list of his complaints

19. In addition to formal supervision, every group of officers soon develops informal leaders who influence the other members of the group. 19.____
Of the following statements about informal leaders, the one that is GENERALLY correct is that they

A. provide supervision when the regular supervisor is absent
B. are entitled to special benefits for their services
C. can be used to help settle disputes between employees
D. prevent the rapid transmission of orders

20. The grapevine is a frequently used means of informal communication in any work location. 20.____
The one of the following statements that BEST describes the attitude a superior officer should take in relation to the grapevine is that it is

A. unreliable and should not be trusted
B. useful and should be recognized
C. valuable and should be the chief method of transmitting orders
D. insignificant and should be ignored

21. As a supervising officer, it may be useful for you to conduct periodic interviews with each of your subordinates to discuss his job performance in broad perspective. 21.____
All of the following are ground rules to follow during such an interview EXCEPT

A. showing him how he compares in work performance with other supervisors in your district
B. giving him a chance to talk
C. focusing on what can be learned from any mistakes discussed rather than on the mistakes themselves
D. avoiding a discussion of personalities

22. When you, as a superior officer, are correcting the errors of a supervisor in your district, which of the following is NOT a good point to keep in mind? 22.____

A. Find something on which to compliment the supervisor before you correct him
B. Watch yourself carefully to avoid the mistake of overcorrecting
C. Correct the supervisor at the same time as you correct other supervisors who make similar mistakes
D. Induce the supervisor to correct himself if possible

23. Following are four steps to be used when instructing a subordinate in the performance of his job: 23.____

I. Observe the subordinate doing the job
II. Compare his performance to established standards
III. Explain the purpose of the job to the subordinate
IV. Demonstrate each step of the job

Which of the following choices lists the CORRECT order in which the above steps should be taken?

A. III, IV, I, II
B. IV, III, I, II
C. III, IV, II, I
D. IV, III, II, I

24. Of the following leadership characteristics, the one that is generally considered PRIMARY for a supervisor is the ability to 24.____

A. achieve good working relations with fellow supervisors
B. get subordinates to air their personal problems
C. take action to get the job done
D. plan his work efficiently

25. A recently appointed supervising officer is placed in charge of a district which includes several senior employees. He finds that while these subordinates are able to learn new tasks and methods, some of them tend to take longer to learn procedural changes than newer, younger workers. 25.____
Of the following, the MAIN reason for this is that senior workers

A. are embarrassed by younger workers' intelligence
B. have to *unlearn* what was taught them in the past
C. form learning blocks when they are supervised by a younger person
D. are more interested in doing the work than in academic discussion

KEY (CORRECT ANSWERS)

1.	D	11.	A
2.	C	12.	C
3.	D	13.	B
4.	C	14.	C
5.	A	15.	A
6.	A	16.	A
7.	D	17.	B
8.	B	18.	D
9.	B	19.	C
10.	C	20.	B

21. A
22. C
23. A
24. C
25. B

EXAMINATION SECTION
TEST 1

DIRECTIONS: Each question or incomplete statement is followed by several suggested answers or completions. Select the one that BEST answers the question or completes the statement. *PRINT THE LETTER OF THE CORRECT ANSWER IN THE SPACE AT THE RIGHT.*

1. When training your subordinates in a new method of crowd control, which one of the following techniques SHOULD be used? 1.____

   A. Teach them the whole job at one time, whether it contains a great many steps or only a few
   B. Issue orders without giving reasons because this will result in more questions and delays
   C. Explain and demonstrate, one step at a time
   D. Use technical language in order to make instructions precise

2. It is sometimes necessary to provide additional training for staff members who are poor in their performance of specific tasks. 2.____
   Of the following, the MOST effective way of improving staff performance is to

   A. use visual aids along with reading material to train staff on the general subject involved
   B. train subordinates to perform only those tasks which they normally perform
   C. plan and carry out programs to meet the subordinates' real work needs
   D. provide training only for staff members performing critical tasks

3. Assume that as a superior officer you confront one of your subordinate officers with the fact that he is not performing his job effectively. The officer tries to avoid the blame and shifts the criticism to other officers including yourself. 3.____
   Which one of the following is NOT a good way of handling this situation?

   A. Speaking and acting in an impartial and fair-minded manner
   B. Trying to determine why the officer finds it difficult to accept justifiable criticism
   C. Calling in the other officers whom this subordinate has criticized and having them discuss the matter with him
   D. Listening to the officer, at least at the outset, rather than interrupting his statement

4. For a superior officer to discuss a subordinate's performance evaluation with him is GENERALLY 4.____

   A. *inadvisable;* such a discussion will discourage a good worker
   B. *advisable;* the subordinate must know about the quality of his performance for improvement to occur
   C. *inadvisable;* a good performance evaluation will result in the subordinate's asking for more responsibility
   D. *advisable;* such discussions generally lead to a change in the subordinate's evaluation

5. The one of the following which is the MAJOR cause of employee lateness is 5.____

A. low morale
B. excessive fatigue
C. accidents
D. sickness

6. For officers to work together smoothly, teamwork is necessary .
Which one of the following statements BEST describes the relationship between leadership and teamwork? 6.____

A. Leadership cannot exist without teamwork.
B. Teamwork cannot exist without leadership.
C. Leadership and teamwork are one and the same.
D. There is no relationship between leadership and teamwork.

7. For superiors who wish to achieve proper discipline among subordinates, it is generally MOST difficult to 7.____

A. obtain rapid compliance with orders and directives
B. prevent subordinates from questioning orders that are issued to them
C. achieve compliance with orders while encouraging individual initiative
D. use punishment to prevent infractions of the rules

8. Of the following, it is MOST likely that laxity in administering discipline will result in 8.____

A. a loss of respect for their superior on the part of subordinates
B. the satisfactory completion of the organization's job
C. an increase in the number of disturbances at centers
D. the establishment of proper conditions for successful administration

9. In dealing with a subordinate who shows a lack of interest in performing his duties, a superior officer should GENERALLY 9.____

A. assign to him all the difficult work
B. give him more responsibility
C. inspect his performance more often than usual
D. give him direct, detailed orders

10. A superior officer who has a highly motivated group of officers under his command GENERALLY 10.____

A. shows an interest in how they are doing and is willing to back them up
B. spends most of his time in closely supervising his subordinates
C. supervises mainly through one of his subordinate officers
D. is management-oriented rather than subordinate-oriented

11. As a superior, you might have to supervise subordinate officers who are very enthusiastic and ambitious.
Which one of the following is the BEST reason for carefully watching the work of such officers?
They 11.____

A. may produce so much work that other officers resent them
B. may appear to be overly concerned about being promoted
C. might make decisions before obtaining the necessary information
D. may be seeking the superior's job

12. In dealing with the public, officers should behave with courtesy. 12.____
Which one of the following practices would be LEAST effective in promoting courtesy?

A. Giving advice on subjects about which you are not well informed
B. Learning to take constructive criticism intelligently
C. Avoiding discussions of a personal nature
D. Treating members of the public as you would like to be treated

13. When directing the officers under your command, which one of the following is generally the MOST effective method of supervision? 13.____

A. Provide your directions through written orders to prevent misunderstanding
B. Supervise every detail of the work closely so that it is carried out exactly as you want it
C. Limit your concern to getting the job done and not to the people doing the work
D. Set up general standards and goals so that officers have leeway as to how to achieve them

14. Leadership is particularly important in the security field. 14.____
Of the following, people GENERALLY expect their leader to

A. state, *Do as I say, not as I do*
B. refuse to allow changes in orders
C. get many of his ideas from his subordinates
D. take his feelings out on those who make mistakes

15. The MOST important single factor in the selection of a person for assignment to a position of greater responsibility should be his 15.____

A. demonstrated ability to do the job
B. schooling, both civilian and military
C. training and experience on the job
D. length of service

16. Security training received by security officers and noted in their personnel charts or records should NOT be used as a basis for 16.____

A. indicating individual degrees of skill
B. assigning officers to particular shifts
C. establishing priorities of instruction
D. presenting a consolidated picture of the training status

17. As a superior officer, you note that one of your subordinates has not been performing his job properly. You discover that the cause of this problem seems to be that he drinks excessively when off duty. 17.____
Of the following, the BEST way to handle this situation is to

A. discipline the officer to the fullest extent possible
B. discuss the problem and possible solutions with the officer's fellow workers
C. wait until the officer has straightened himself out and then counsel him
D. have a blunt and firm talk with the officer and direct him to seek treatment

18. Officers who are overly sensitive to criticism are one of the problems that superiors must deal with. 18.____
Of the following, which is the BEST way to handle such officers?
They should

A. not be talked to differently from other officers
B. be criticized only on serious mistakes
C. not be criticized at all
D. be reassured of their worth to their unit

19. A superior officer who suspects an employee of petty office theft calls the employee to his office and questions him directly. 19.____
In this situation, the superior's action is

A. *desirable,* primarily because the subordinate should be allowed to answer these accusations privately
B. *desirable,* primarily because confrontation will persuade the employee to tell the truth
C. *undesirable,* primarily because line department personnel should handle such matters
D. *undesirable,* primarily because direct confrontation might unnecessarily embarrass the employee

20. Assume that a certain superior officer assigns a task, without explanation, to a new subordinate who is not yet accepted by the work group. 20.____
Of the following, the MOST likely result of this action would be to

A. encourage the subordinate to perform at his best
B. make the subordinate feel insecure about proving himself
C. stimulate other officers to do their best to impress the new staff member
D. cause the experienced officers to feel inferior

21. A newly appointed superior officer often faces the problem of supervising officers who were formerly close personal friends of his. 21.____
In this situation, the one of the following which is the BEST approach to take toward these officers is to

A. break all ties with former friends
B. stay personally close with friends as this is always an advantage on the job
C. maintain a relationship of easy, occasional familiarity
D. become businesslike on the job but remain close socially

22. Assume that you, as a superior officer, are talking over a proposed change in procedure with your subordinates which would require their full cooperation. 22.____
Which one of the following actions would be MOST appropriate for you to take if your subordinates suggest modifications in the procedure?

A. Prepare arguments against your subordinates' suggestions while you are listening to them
B. Refuse to accept suggestions for changes since procedures can't be modified
C. Listen carefully since your subordinates' suggestions may have merit
D. Accept the recommendations of your more experienced subordinates

23. The successful supervisor should be aware that two of his most important assets are patience and understanding. 23.____
Of the following actions by a supervisor, the one that is LEAST likely to demonstrate these qualities would be to

A. make deadlines realistic and reachable
B. reprimand an employee the minute he makes a mistake
C. assist employees in work-related problems
D. discuss changes in procedures with subordinates

24. One of a supervisor's goals should be to create and maintain a force of loyal subordinates with high morale. This objective is likely to be achieved by all of the following EXCEPT 24.____

A. making subordinate officers feel that their job is an important one
B. encouraging supervisors to be concerned with the individual needs of subordinates
C. giving subordinate officers an opportunity to express their thoughts, likes, and interests to their supervisors
D. having supervisors rely only on the advice of trusted employees when resolving disputes between subordinates

25. One of a supervisor's major responsibilities is to evaluate the performance of his subordinates. 25.____
Which one of the following practices would be LEAST productive in developing meaningful evaluations from performance interviews?

A. Make positive statements only
B. Outline the points to discuss
C. Adjust to the individual and situation
D. Allow the employee to participate

KEY (CORRECT ANSWERS)

1. C
2. C
3. C
4. B
5. A

6. B
7. C
8. A
9. B
10. A

11. C
12. A
13. D
14. C
15. A

16. B
17. D
18. D
19. A
20. B

21. C
22. C
23. B
24. D
25. A

TEST 2

DIRECTIONS: Each question or incomplete statement is followed by several suggested answers or completions. Select the one that BEST answers the question or completes the statement. *PRINT THE LETTER OF THE COREECT ANSWER IN THE SPACE AT THE RIGHT.*

1. Assume that you are a superior officer concerned with improving the attitude of your subordinates toward their work. 1.____
Of the following, the action that is MOST likely to improve this attitude would be for you to

   A. allow your subordinates to take extra time off
   B. interpret rules and regulations leniently
   C. request a merit increase in salary for your subordinates
   D. train your subordinates to perform at the highest possible level

2. Assume that two of the officers under your command are hotly disputing the accuracy of a log book entry. One of the officers asks for your opinion. 2.____
Which of the following would be LEAST advisable for you to do in this situation?

   A. Ask the officers to present their views calmly
   B. Keep your temper and remain impartial
   C. Stop the argument and then give your decision
   D. Judge the argument in proportion to its importance

3. A superior officer notices that one of his subordinates is not doing his job. 3.____
In this situation, it would be MOST appropriate for the superior officer to

   A. caution the subordinate officer promptly
   B. ignore the incident this time
   C. check on the subordinate officer's behavior in an hour
   D. warn the subordinate officer at the end of his work day that a report may be filed

4. A recently appointed superior officer finds it difficult to make the decisions required in his new position. 4.____
Which one of the following suggestions would be MOST helpful to him in overcoming this problem?

   A. Don't be concerned because everyone makes mistakes, and any mistake caused by your decisions will be ignored.
   B. Remember that you will be judged by the long range soundness of all of your decisions.
   C. Since you are now in charge of a number of officers, let them bear the decision-making responsibility.
   D. Remember that you have a superior and that he can make the decision for you.

5. Of the following, the BEST reason for a superior officer to nake inspections and rounds is to 5.____

   A. observe the physical appearance of personnel
   B. determine whether communication equipment is working properly

C. decide whether adequate records are being kept
D. see that the performance of subordinates conforms with departmental standards

6. Assume that you, as a superior officer, have made an inspection and have submitted recommendations for improvements. 6.____
Which one of the following actions should be taken to assure that the desired results are obtained from the inspection?
You should

A. distribute copies of the recommendations to all members of the force
B. follow-up to determine whether the recommended improvements have been made
C. give credit to other officers when it is due in order to help increase morale
D. set up a schedule so that you inspect once a week

7. Assume that you have noticed that one of your subordinates has been quiet and rather depressed for two to three days with no change in his usual satisfactory job performance. 7.____
Of the following, the BEST action for you to take in this situation is to

A. ask him to describe his feelings in detail
B. act as if you noticed no change in the subordinate's behavior
C. tell him to forget what's bothering him
D. recommend that he seek professional guidance

8. Assume that you wish to introduce a change in your subordinates' work procedures in order to improve their performance. 8.____
Of the following, the BEST way to gain acceptance of this change is for you to

A. stress its positive aspects
B. downgrade past practices
C. delay discussing it for a while
D. order your subordinates to follow the new procedure at once

9. Suppose you come across two of your subordinate officers having an argument about the boundaries of their patrol posts. 9.____
Which of the following is the LEAST advisable course of action for you to take after stopping the argument?

A. Tell the officers to speak with you individually
B. Have the officers submit their views in writing for you to evaluate properly when you have time
C. Meet with both officers in your office after they finish their tours
D. Tell the officers to consult you on such matters in the future

10. Assume that a superior officer is explaining a new rule to his men at roll call. One officer states that he does not like the rule. The superior tells the officer that he agrees with him, but that the rule must be followed anyway. In this situation, the superior officer's statement was 10.____

A. *proper,* chiefly because the men should know where superiors stand on rules and regulations
B. *improper,* chiefly because superiors should not indicate disagreement with a change in rules since they must enforce them

C. *proper,* chiefly because efficiency improves when supervisors and subordinates agree on new rules
D. *improper,* chiefly because questions regarding rule changes should be answered at staff meetings rather than at roll call

11. Assume that you find that several of your subordinate officers have not performed satisfactorily during the last few emergency situations at your work location. The one of the following actions which is LEAST likely to improve their performance is for you to 11.____

A. keep the subordinates informed about how they performed after each emergency
B. stay alert for officers who are having difficulty with their work
C. circulate among the officers at emergencies
D. avoid the use of criticism

12. Of the following qualifications for an officer, the one that is MOST important is the ability to 12.____

A. understand and get along with people
B. write a good report
C. overcome resistance to arrest
D. solve crimes

13. Assume that you have noticed that one of your subordinate officers makes errors when questioning clients. You discuss with him the proper method to use when questioning clients.
Of the following, your NEXT step should be to 13.____

A. ask another officer to check on your subordinate's procedure when questioning clients
B. tell the officer to discuss with others how they question clients
C. have the officer report regularly to you about the clients he questions
D. watch the officer to see how he questions clients

14. One of the MOST important rules to follow when communicating with your superior is: 14.____

A. Report everything that happens at your work location to him
B. Pass on to him rumors and gossip heard within your center
C. Let him hear from you first about any unusual success, problem or error
D. Assign to one of your subordinates the responsibility of communicating with your supervisor

15. A superior officer may be required to instruct subordinates in the performance of their tasks.
Which of the following would NOT be proper when instructing a small group of employees? 15.____

A. Use simple language
B. Explain the procedure and the reason for the procedure
C. Demonstrate one step at a time
D. Use the lecture method instead of the discussion method whenever possible

16. Assume that a new officer has joined your unit. Which of the following approaches should you, as his superior officer, use in introducing him to the job? 16.____

    A. Put him right to work; he will learn best through his mistakes
    B. Act sternly, thereby gaining his respect and indicating the proper supervisor-subordinate relationship
    C. Give him the overall picture of the department and unit he is in
    D. Praise him, even when he makes errors, in order to gain his confidence

17. When a new officer begins work, he will often perform tasks ineffectively, thus requiring corrective action by his supervisor. 17.____
    In this situation, which one of the following represents the MOST desirable course of action for the supervisor?

    A. Point out specific errors in performance and how to correct them
    B. Tell the new officer that he is not doing the job properly and assign him to a new task
    C. Avoid criticism in the beginning since it may result in bitterness
    D. Do not criticize because criticism is not currently considered an acceptable tool of management

18. Of the following types of work, the one that is MOST likely to lead to dissatisfaction is work that is 18.____

    A. difficult to perform
    B. tiring to complete
    C. uncomplicated
    D. unimportant

19. When instructing subordinates to perform new tasks, the one of the following that is LEAST important in helping then to learn is to 19.____

    A. explain the procedure to them in a step-by-step manner
    B. show them what they must do
    C. let them do the task under guidance
    D. have them perform the task without supervision so they may learn from their mistakes

20. Which one of the following is the MOST important single thing to bear in mind about giving orders? 20.____

    A. An order should be given to a capable employee, not an uncooperative one.
    B. If an order is given correctly, you will not have to check the work.
    C. An order should be given in as forceful a manner as possible to assure that it is understood.
    D. An order is given because it is necessary to bring about certain results.

21. Suppose that a subordinate asks you about a rumor he has heard. The rumor deals with a subject which your superiors consider *confidential*. 21.____
    Which of the following BEST describes how you should answer the officer?
    Tell

    A. the officer that you don't make the rules and that he should speak to higher ranking officers
    B. the officer that you will ask your superior for information

C. him only that you cannot comment on the matter
D. him the rumor is not true

22. Superior officers often find it difficult to *get their message across* when instructing newly appointed officers in their various duties. 22.____
The MAIN reason for this is generally that the

A. duties of the officers have increased
B. superior officer is often so expert in his area that he fails to see it from the learner's point of view
C. superior officer adapts his instruction to the slowest learner in the group
D. new officers are younger, less concerned with job security, and more interested in fringe benefits

23. Assume that you are discussing a security problem with an officer under your command. During the discussion, you see that the officer's eyes are turning away from you and that he is not paying attention. 23.____
In order to get the officer's attention, you should FIRST

A. ask him to look you in the eye
B. talk to him about sports
C. tell him he is being very rude
D. change your tone of voice

24. As a superior officer, you may find it necessary to conduct meetings with your subordinates. 24.____
Of the following, which would be MOST helpful in assuring that a meeting accomplishes the purpose for which it was called?

A. Give notice of the conclusions you would like to reach at the start of the meeting
B. Delay the start of the meeting until everyone is present
C. Write down points to be discussed in proper sequence
D. Make sure everyone is clear on whatever conclusions have been reached and on what must be done after the meeting

25. Every superior officer will occasionally be called upon to deliver a reprimand to a subordinate. If done properly, this can greatly help an officer improve his performance. 25.____
Which one of the following is NOT a good practice to follow when giving a reprimand?

A. Maintain your composure and temper
B. Reprimand a subordinate in the presence of other officers so they can learn the same lesson
C. Try to understand why the officer was not able to perform satisfactorily
D. Let your knowledge of the officer involved determine the exact nature of the reprimand

KEY (CORRECT ANSWERS)

1.	D	11.	D
2.	C	12.	A
3.	A	13.	D
4.	B	14.	C
5.	D	15.	D
6.	B	16.	C
7.	B	17.	A
8.	A	18.	D
9.	B	19.	D
10.	B	20.	D

21. B
22. B
23. D
24. D
25. B

TEST 3

DIRECTIONS: Each question or incomplete statement is followed by several suggested answers or completions. Select the one that BEST answers the question or completes the statement. *PRINT THE LETTER OF THE CORRECT ANSWER IN THE SPACE AT THE RIGHT.*

1. Of the following, the PRIMARY purpose of communications between subordinates and superiors is to 1.____

   A. develop language skills
   B. enable subordinates to air their grievances
   C. help establish friendly ties
   D. solve job problems

2. Of the following, the MOST necessary elements of good communication are 2.____

   A. openness and form
   B. details and subjectivity
   C. speed and dependability
   D. length and appearance

3. Of the following, the MOST important role of a supervisor is that of 3.____

   A. being able to understand how his men feel about their assignments
   B. establishing good contacts with the administration
   C. fulfilling his responsibility to the assigned position
   D. presenting a good public image on the behalf of his organization

4. Of the following, the LEAST desirable behavior of a senior officer would be for him to 4.____

   A. attempt to gain the respect of superiors
   B. attempt to find causes of high employee turnover
   C. ignore infrequent latenesses
   D. ignore suggestions which may prove unworthy

5. A senior officer who consults with his subordinates about operational planning is GENERALLY 5.____

   A. attempting to prove his supervisory ability
   B. developing their job participation and cooperation
   C. passing down his responsibilities to others
   D. searching for an employee with supervisory ability

6. If a senior officer conducted supervision and inspection programs in order to become aware of his men's conduct, he would GENERALLY be considered to be 6.____

   A. excessively strict and authoritarian
   B. looking for potential troublemakers
   C. overconscientious in his work
   D. performing a vital duty

7. Of the following, the BEST reason for a supervisor's evaluation of his own on-the-job performance is to enable him to 7.____

   A. find the best methods of supervising his men and in getting the job done
   B. give the impression that he is sincere in trying to become a better supervisor

C. make a favorable impression on his superiors
D. make his work seem more important than it actually is

8. Assume that you are a senior officer making a performance evaluation of an officer. The reason for NOT drawing conclusions too quickly is CHIEFLY that 8.____

A. without due consideration of all the facts, you are likely to evaluate the officer on biased personal judgment
B. evaluation reports take a great deal of time and thought
C. senior officers must consult with superiors before drawing conclusions about a subordinate's performance
D. the officer might try to disprove any wrong information which you may have obtained about him

9. A senior officer notices two officers, known to be good workers, playing practical jokes and pranks on the other employees. 9.____
In this case, disciplinary action is

A. *desirable,* chiefly because horseplay on the job is not, strictly speaking, against the rules
B. *undesirable,* chiefly because good workers tend to correct their own improper actions
C. *desirable,* chiefly because horseplay could provoke other employees and that would disrupt normal work routine
D. *undesirable,* chiefly because a supervisor should not get involved with employees' affairs

10. Resistance to or resentment of training is likely to be an attitude shown by many officers. Therefore, it is important for a senior officer to understand the causes of his men's attitudes and learn how to deal with them. Of the following, which is the BEST method of lessening an officer's resentment of training? 10.____

A. Give the officers extra time off for taking part in the training program
B. Openly criticize the officer who often makes mistakes during training
C. Recommend promotions for those who complete the training program quickest
D. Explain that the purpose of the training is to help them perform their jobs more efficiently

11. A senior officer required all officers under his supervision to submit a weekly report based on information from their daily log (memo) entries. The senior officer did not examine these reports, but he did file them as proof that the officers were not *sleeping* on the job. 11.____
In general, this practice of the senior officer is considered

A. *correct,* chiefly because the senior officer has little need of the reports since he is usually on the scene to observe the performance of his men
B. *incorrect*, chiefly because, if the senior officer asked for reports, he should read or use the information they contain
C. *correct,* chiefly because any information an officer had could only be based on daily occurrences
D. *incorrect*, chiefly because the senior officer is placing too much emphasis on accuracy of paper work

12. Selecting an employee to be trained for performing the supervisor's duties is generally considered 12.____

A. *desirable*, chiefly because it allows the supervisor to avoid many of his duties
B. *undesirable*, chiefly because it creates the impression that the supervisor is showing favoritism
C. *desirable*, chiefly because supervisory coverage is assured in the absence of the supervisor
D. *undesirable*, chiefly because the trainee will cause the supervisor to worry about possible competition and thus neglect the performance of his duties

13. When discussing lateness with an employee, a supervisor should take the employee to an area where the problem can be discussed privately 13.____
Generally, this practice is considered

A. *desirable,* chiefly because it gives the employee an opportunity to converse with the supervisor in a very casual way
B. *desirable,* chiefly because it keeps the problem from being discussed in front of an audience
C. *undesirable,* chiefly because isolating an employee from his co-workers causes the *rumor-mongers* to spread false gossip about the matter
D. *undesirable,* chiefly because trivial matters can be mentioned in the open without any repercussions

14. When an officer shows a pattern of abuse in his use of sick leave, a senior officer should 14.____

A. ask the officer for medical proof of all future illnesses
B. discourage other officers from abusing sick leave by giving the offending officer a public warning
C. interview the officer and inquire about the reasons for his behavior
D. acknowledge the officer's right to sick leave as set forth in departmental rules and regulations

15. Of the following, the MAJOR reason why grapevines generally develop in an agency is that 15.____

A. employees have too much idle time
B. employees want to socialize and gossip with other employees while working
C. superior officers avoid reporting bad news downward from management to subordinates
D. there is a communication gap between management and employees

16. If a newly-assigned senior officer is doubtful about the exact details of the assignment he is about to give to an officer, he should GENERALLY 16.____

A. ask to speak to the officer in private and give him another assignment
B. delay giving the assignment until he clears up his own doubt
C. attempt to explain to the officer what he knows about the assignment in the best possible way
D. put the assignment in writing

17. Of the following situations, which one would justify a supervisor's giving direct orders to another supervisor's subordinate? 17.____

    A. A supervisor away from his normal assignment observes a serious disturbance and gives orders to the officers in that area.
    B. A supervisor foresees a problem that will arise the next day in another district and immediately proceeds to inform the other supervisor's officers of the action they should take.
    C. A supervisor tells an officer under another supervisor to perform a duty a week from today because he feels it is an urgent matter.
    D. None of the above situations would justify direct supervision by any senior officer.

18. In the planning process, which of the following is NOT a recommended practice in preparing your final plan of action? 18.____

    A. Obtain all important available facts related to the problem
    B. Clarify the problem before any plan is created
    C. Make the plan easy to understand so that it can be carried out efficiently
    D. Never make assumptions or forecasts about what could occur

19. Of the following, the BEST way for a senior officer to get his subordinates to carry out his orders is to 19.____

    A. explain whenever possible why the orders are being given
    B. let subordinates know in advance the penalties for disobeying his orders
    C. describe the steps that must be followed in performing each order
    D. issue all orders in the form of direct and positive commands

20. It is MOST correct to state that race prejudice is to the GREATEST extent 20.____

    A. an inborn human characteristic
    B. the result of training and group association
    C. the product of ghetto areas
    D. a condition limited to adults only

21. *Scapegoating* is a form of prejudice which results MAINLY from 21.____

    A. degrading minority groups in an effort to secure status for one's own group
    B. shifting the blame for social inadequacies and ills from oneself to others
    C. thinking of people not as individual persons but rather placing them in carelessly formed, all-embracing classifications
    D. maintaining the existing order to prevent other groups from rising in social and economic status

22. The MOST important step in democratic supervision is 22.____

    A. allowing the employee a chance to apologize whenever he makes an error
    B. keeping tight control over employees
    C. making the employee realize that he needs your approval in order to keep his position
    D. showing an interest in the welfare of the employee

23. Evaluating a subordinate's likes and dislikes concerning his work is GENERALLY considered to be 23.____

A. valuable in assigning work details to the subordinate
B. necessary only when the subordinate complains of dissatisfaction with his daily duties
C. unnecessary and a waste of time
D. useful only in establishing a good relationship with the subordinate

24. Employee motivation is very critical in keeping up the morale of employees. 24.____
Of the following, which is generally the BEST method of supervision which both motivates and maintains high morale?

A. Aid employees in finding satisfaction in their assignments even if it requires extra time and responsibility
B. Allow employees to work with a free hand and without daily interruptions
C. Don't get involved or become concerned with interests or problems of employees outside the job
D. Prove your friendship to a select number of employees so that the remainder of the staff will feel you are a *good guy* to work for

25. When attempting to motivate an experienced individual, it is BEST for a senior officer to appeal to the person's 25.____

A. emotions
B. positive interests
C. negative feelings
D. inhibitions

KEY (CORRECT ANSWERS)

1. D
2. C
3. C
4. D
5. B
6. D
7. A
8. A
9. C
10. D
11. B
12. C
13. B
14. C
15. D
16. B
17. A
18. D
19. A
20. B
21. B
22. D
23. A
24. A
25. B

EVALUATING INFORMATION AND EVIDENCE
EXAMINATION SECTION
TEST 1

DIRECTIONS: Each question or incomplete statement is followed by several suggested answers or completions. Select the one that BEST answers the question or completes the statement. *PRINT THE LETTER OF THE CORRECT ANSWER IN THE SPACE AT THE RIGHT.*

Questions 1-4.

DIRECTIONS: Questions 1 to 4 measure your ability (1) to determine whether statements from witnesses say essentially the same thing and (2) to determine the evidence needed to make it reasonably certain that a particular conclusion is true.

To do well in this part of the test, you do NOT have to have a working knowledge of police procedures and techniques or to have any more familiarity with crimes and criminal behavior than that acquired from reading newspapers, listening to radio, or watching TV. To do well in this part, you must read carefully and reason closely. Sloppy reading or sloppy reasoning will lead to a low score.

1. In which of the following do the two statements made say essentially the same thing in two different ways? 1.____
   I. All members of the pro-x group are free from persecution. No person that is persecuted is a member of the pro-x group.
   II. Some responsible employees of the police department are not supervisors. Some police department supervisors are not responsible employees.

   The CORRECT answer is:

   A. I *only* B. II *only*
   C. Both I and II D. Neither I nor II

2. In which of the following do the two statements made say essentially the same thing in two different ways? 2.____
   I. All Nassau County police officers weigh less than 225 pounds.
   II. No police officer weighs more than 225 pounds.
   No police officer is an alcoholic. No alcoholic is a police officer.

   The CORRECT answer is:

   A. I *only* B. II *only*
   C. Both I and II D. Neither I nor II

3. Summary of Evidence Collected to Date: All pimps in the precinct own pink-colored cars and carry knives. 3.____
   Prematurely Drawn Conclusion: Any person in the precinct who carries a knife is a pimp.
   Which one of the following additional pieces of evidence, if any, would make it *reasonably certain* that the conclusion drawn is TRUE?

   A. Each person who carries a knife owns a pink-colored car.
   B. All persons who own pink-colored cars pimp.

C. No one who carries a knife has a vocation other than pimping.
D. None of these

4. Summary of Evidence Collected to Date: 4.____
   1. Some of the robbery suspects have served time as convicted felons.
   2. Some of the robbery suspects are female.

   Prematurely Drawn Conclusion: Some of the female suspects have never served time as convicted felons.
   Which one of the following additional pieces of evidence, if any, would make it *reasonably certain* that the conclusion drawn is TRUE?

   A. The number of female suspects is the same as the number of robbery suspects who have served time as convicted felons.
   B. The number of female suspects is smaller than the number of convicted felons.
   C. The number of suspects that have served time is smaller than the number of suspects that have been convicted of a felony.
   D. None of these

Questions 5-8.

DIRECTIONS: Questions 5 to 8 measure your ability to orient yourself within a given section of a town, neighborhood, or particular area. Each of the questions describes a starting point and a destination. Assume that you are driving a patrol car in the area shown on the map accompanying the questions. Use the map as a basis for choosing the shortest way to get from one point to another without breaking the law.

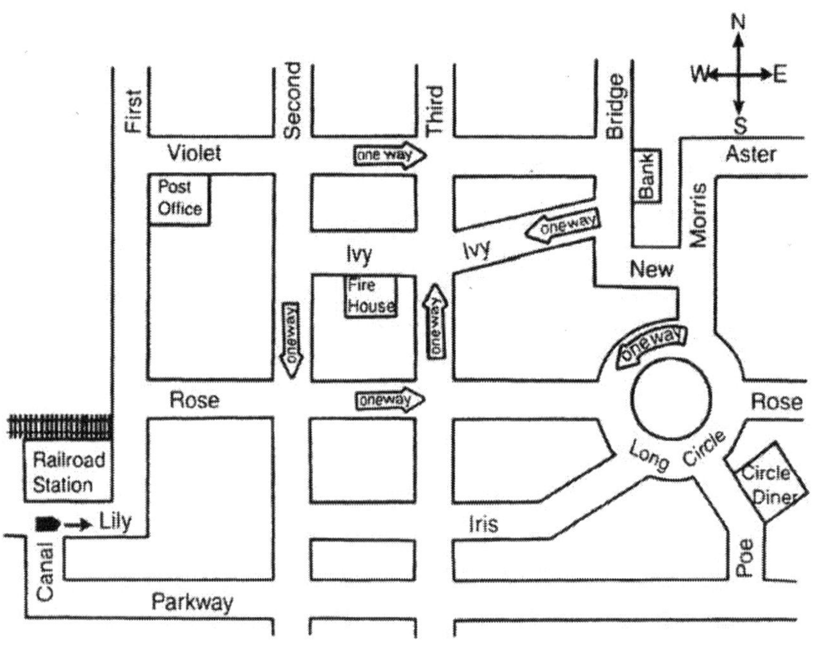

A street marked *one way* is one-way for the full length, even when there are breaks or jogs in the street. EXCEPTION: A street that does not have the same name over the full length.

5. A patrol car at the train station is sent to the bank to investigate a robbery. The SHORTEST way to get there without breaking any traffic laws is to go 5.____

A. east on Lily, north on First, east on Rose, north on Third, and east on Ivy to bank
B. east on Lily, north on First, east on Violet, and south on Bridge to bank
C. south on Canal, east on Parkway, north on Poe, around Long Circle to Morris, west on New, and north on Bridge to bank
D. south on Canal, east on Parkway, north on Third, and east on Ivy to bank

6. At the bank, the patrol car receives a call to hurry to the post office. The SHORTEST way to get there without breaking any traffic laws is to go 6.____

A. west on Ivy, south on Second, west on Rose, and north on First to post office
B. west on Ivy, south on Second, west on Rose, and south on First to post office
C. south on Bridge, east on New, south on Morris, around Long Circle, south on Poe, west on Parkway, north on Canal, east on Lily, and north on First to post office
D. north on Bridge, west on Violet, and south on First to post office.

7. On leaving the post office, the police officers decide to go to the Circle Diner. The SHORTEST way to get there without breaking any traffic laws is to go 7.____

A. south on First, left on Rose, right on Second, left on Parkway, and right on Poe to diner
B. south on First, left on Rose, around Long Circle, and right on Poe to diner
C. south on First, left on Rose, right on Second, right on Iris, around Long Circle, and left on Poe to diner
D. west on Violet, right on Bridge, right on New, right on Morris, around Long Circle, and left on Poe to diner

8. During lunch break, a fire siren sounds and the police officers rush to their patrol car and head for the fire-house. The SHORTEST way to get there without breaking any traffic laws is to go 8.____

A. north on Poe, around Long Circle, west on Iris, north on Third, and west on Ivy to firehouse
B. north on Poe, around Long Circle, north on Morris, west on New, north on Bridge, and west on Ivy to firehouse
C. north on Poe, around Long Circle, west on Rose, north on Third, and west on Ivy to firehouse
D. south on Poe, west on Parkway, north on Third, and east on Ivy to firehouse

Questions 9-13.

DIRECTIONS: Questions 9 to 13 measure your ability to understand written descriptions of events. Each question presents you with a description of an accident, a crime, or an event and asks you which of four drawings BEST represent it.

In the drawings, the following symbols are used (these symbols and their meanings will be repeated in the test):

A moving vehicle is represented by this symbol: (front) ▭ (rear)

A parked vehicle is represented by this symbol: (front) ◀■ (rear)

A pedestrian or a bicyclist is represented by this symbol: •

The path and direction of travel of a vehicle or pedestrian is indicated by a solid line: ⟶

EXCEPTION: The path and direction of travel of each vehicle or person directly involved in a collision from the point of impact is indicated by a dotted line: - - →

9. A driver pulling out from between two parked cars on Magic is struck by a vehicle heading east which turns left onto Maple and flees. 9.____
Which of the following depicts the accident?

A.

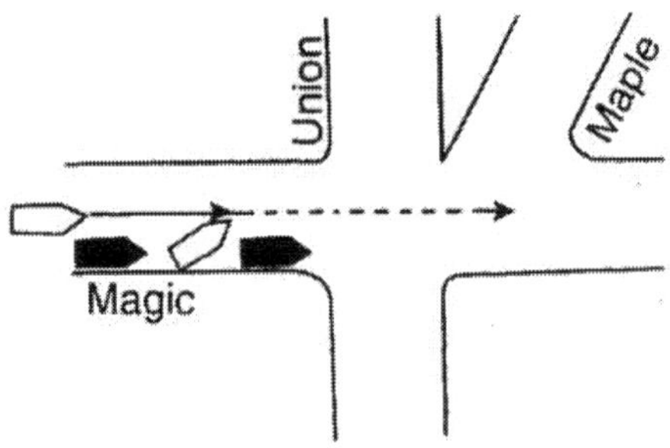

B.

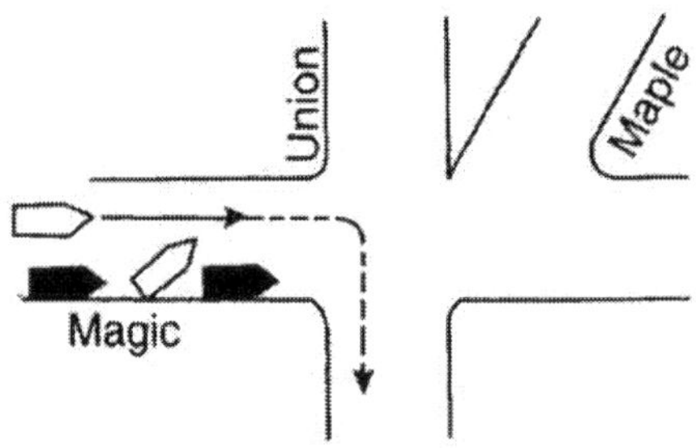

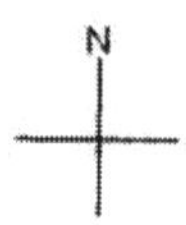

C.

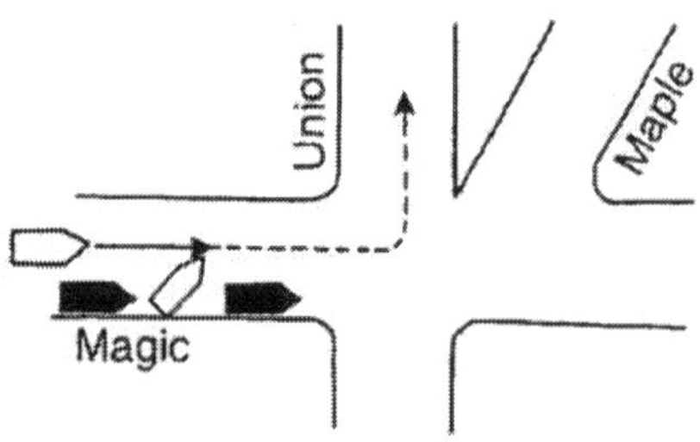

D.

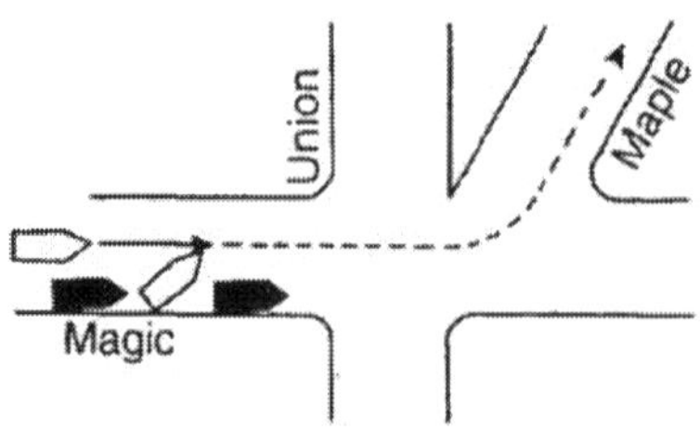

10. As Mr. Jones is driving south on Side. St., he falls asleep at the wheel. His car goes out of control and sideswipes an oncoming car, goes through an intersection, and hits a pedestrian on the southeast corner of Main Street. 10.____
Which of the following depicts the accident?

A.

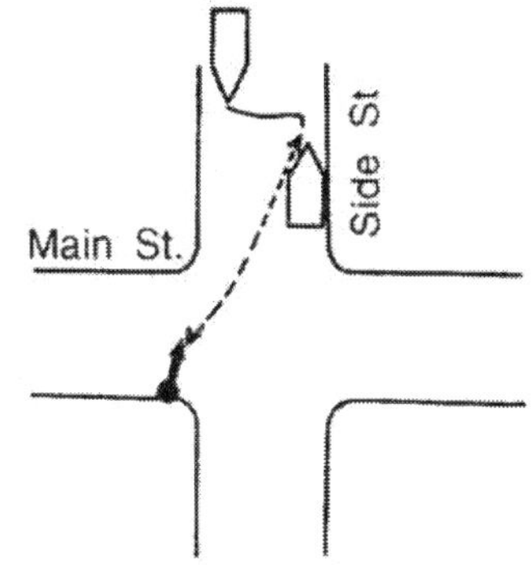

B.

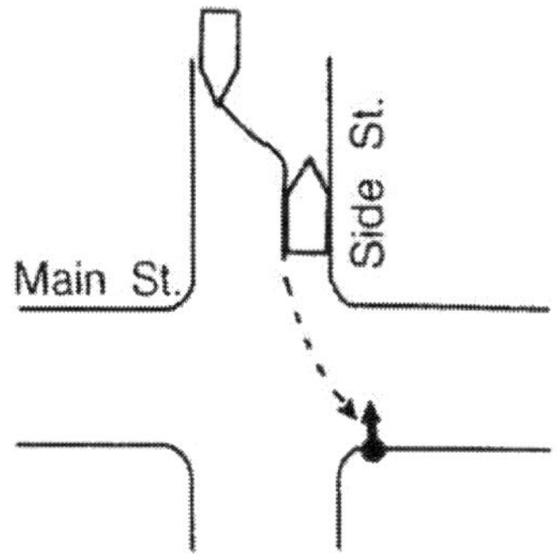

C.

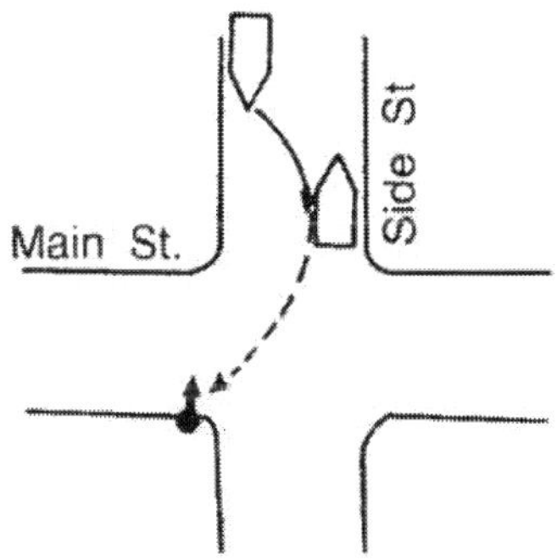

D.

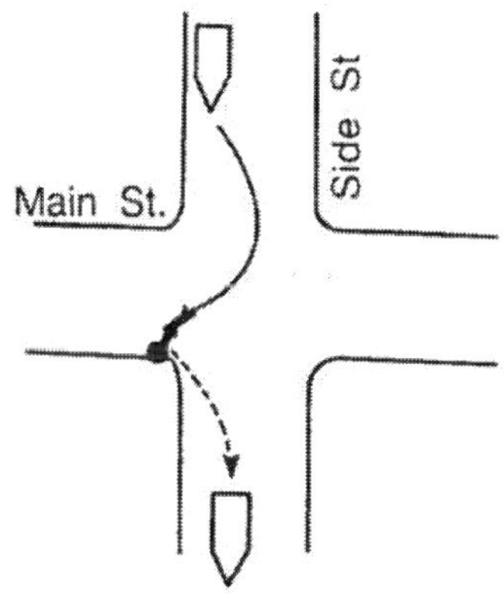

11. A car traveling south on Baltic skids through a red light at the intersection of Baltic and Atlantic, sideswipes a car stopped for a light in the northbound lane, skids 180 degrees, and stops on the west sidewalk of Baltic. 11.____
Which of the following depicts the accident?

A.

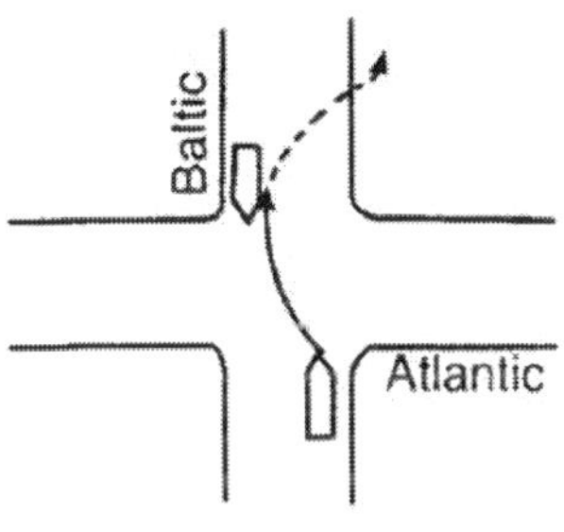

B.

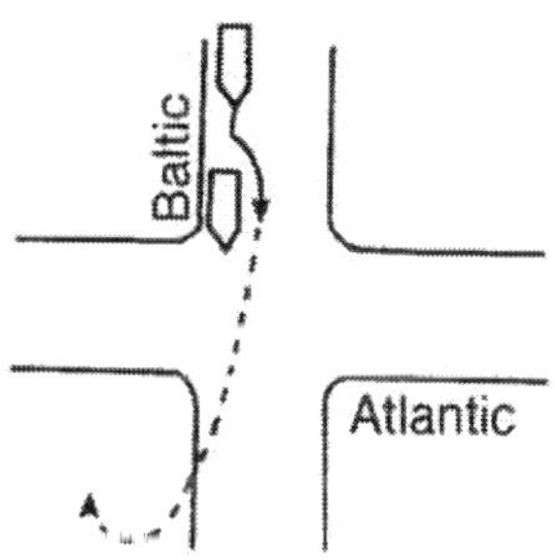

C.

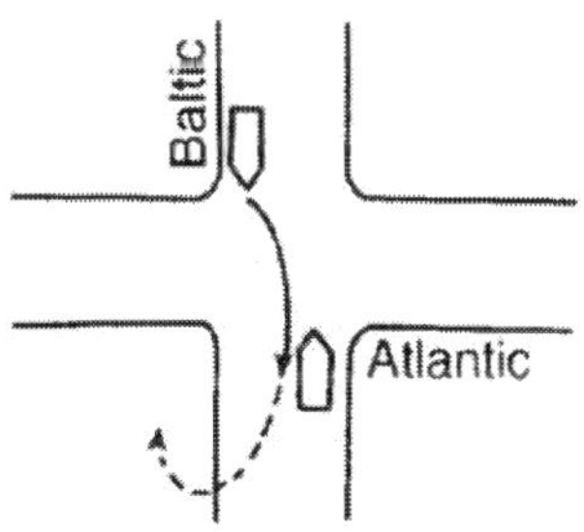

D.

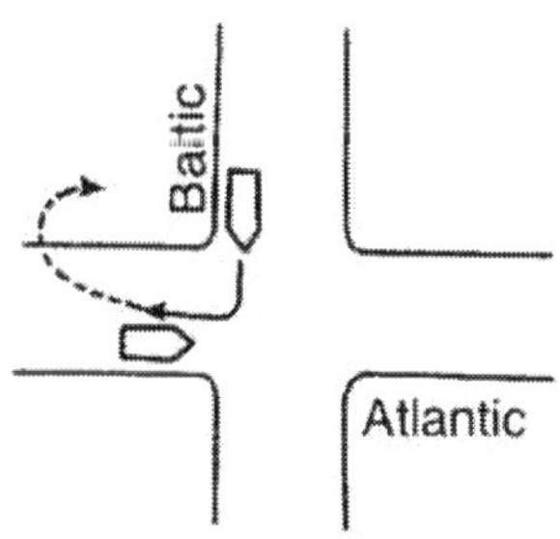

12. When found, the right front end of an automobile was smashed and bent around a post, and the hood was buckled. 12.____
Which of the following cars on a service lot is the car described?

A.

B.

C.

D.

13. An open floor safe with its door bent out of shape was found at the scene. It was empty. An electric drill and several envelopes and papers were found on the floor near the safe. 13.____
Which of the following shows the scene described?

A.

B.

C.

D.

Questions 14-16.

DIRECTIONS: In Questions 14 to 16, you are to pick the word or phrase CLOSEST in meaning to the word or phrase printed in capital letters.

14. HAZARDOUS 14.____

A. uncertain B. threatening C. difficult D. dangerous

15. NEGLIGENT 15.____

A. careless B. fearless C. ruthless D. useless

16. PROVOKE 16.____

A. accuse B. arouse C. insist D. suspend

Questions 17-20.

DIRECTIONS: Questions 17 to 20 measure your ability to do arithmetic related to police work. Each question presents a separate arithmetic problem to be solved.

17. To the nearest hour, how long can a specialized police vehicle with a 40-gallon fuel tank be on the road before heading for a service facility, assuming that the vehicle consumes 8 gallons per hour and must head for a service facility when there are only 8 gallons in the tank? 17.____

A. 3 B. 4 C. 5 D. None of these

18. A man with a history of vagrancy was found dead under a bridge with the following U.S. currency in a band around his belly: 18.____

7 $5 bills
3 $10 bills
11 $20 bills
9 $50 bills
4 $100 bills

What is the total amount of the money that was found in the band?

A. $1,015 B. $1,135 C. $2,710 D. None of these

19. X is 110 dimes. 19.____
Y is 1,111 pennies.
Which of the following statements about the values of X and Y above is TRUE?

A. X is greater than Y.
B. Y is greater than X.
C. X equals Y.
D. The relationship of X to Y cannot be determined from the information given.

20. Which of the following individuals drinking hard liquor in a bar was 21 years old at the time of the incident? 20.____

A. One born August 26, 1989 - Date of incident is March 17, 2010
B. One born January 6, 1989 - Date of incident is New Year's Eve 2009
C. One born 3/17/89 - Date of incident is 2/14/10
D. None of these

KEY (CORRECT ANSWERS)

1.	A	11.	C
2.	B	12.	D
3.	C	13.	B
4.	D	14.	D
5.	B	15.	A
6.	C	16.	B
7.	B	17.	B
8.	B	18.	B
9.	D	19.	B
10.	B	20.	D

EXAMINATION SECTION
TEST 1

DIRECTIONS: Each question or incomplete statement is followed by several suggested answers or completions. Select the one that BEST answers the question or completes the statement. *PRINT THE LETTER OF THE CORRECT ANSWER IN THE SPACE AT THE RIGHT.*

Questions 1-6.

DIRECTIONS: Questions 1 through 6 consist of descriptions of material to which a filing designation must be assigned.

Assume that the matters and cases described in the questions were referred for handling to a government legal office which has its files set up according to these file designations. The file designation consists of a number of characters and punctuation marks as described below.

The first character refers to agencies whose legal work is handled by this office. These agencies are numbered consecutively in the order in which they first submit a matter for attention, and are identified in an alphabetical card index. To date numbers have been assigned to agencies as follows:

Department of Correction 1
Police Department 2
Department of Traffic 3
Department of Consumer Affairs.. 4
Commission on Human Rights 5
Board of Elections 6
Department of Personnel.. 7
Board of Estimate 8

The second character is separated from the first character by a dash. The second character is the last digit of the year in which a particular lawsuit or matter is referred to the legal office.

The third character is separated from the second character by a colon and may consist of either of the following:

I. A sub-number assigned to each lawsuit to which the agency is a party. Lawsuits are numbered consecutively regardless of year. (Lawsuits are brought by or against agency heads rather than agencies themselves, but references are made to agencies for the purpose of simplification.)

or II. A capital letter assigned to each matter other than a lawsuit according to subject, the subject being identified in an alphabetical index. To date, letters have been assigned to subjects as follows:

Citizenship .... A
Discrimination .... B
Residence Requirements C
Civil Service Examinations .... D
Housing .... E
Gambling .... F
Freedom of Religion .... G

These referrals are numbered consecutively regardless of year. The first referral by a particular agency on citizenship, for example, would be designated A1, followed by A2, A3, etc.

If no reference is made in a question as to how many letters involving a certain subject or how many lawsuits have been referred by an agency, assume that it is the first.

For each question, choose the file designation which is MOST appropriate for filing the material described in the question.

1. In January 2010, two candidates in a 2009 civil service examination for positions with the Department of Correction filed a suit against the Department of Personnel seeking to set aside an educational requirement for the title. The Department of Personnel immediately referred the lawsuit to the legal office for handling. 1.____

   A. 1-9:1 B. 1-0:D1 C. 7-9:D1 D. 7-0:1

2. In 2014, the Police Department made its sixth request for an opinion on whether an employee assignment proposed for 2015 could be considered discriminatory. 2.____

   A. 2-5:1-B6 B. 2-4:6 C. 2-4:1-B6 D. 2-4:B6

3. In 2015, a lawsuit was brought by the Bay Island Action Committee against the Board of Estimate in which the plaintiff sought withdrawal of approval of housing for the elderly in the Bay Island area given by the Board in 2015. 3.____

   A. 8-3:1 B. 8-5:1 C. 8-3:B1 D. 8-5:E1

4. In December 2014, community leaders asked the Police Department to ban outdoor meetings of a religious group on the grounds that the meetings were disrupting the area. Such meetings had been held from time to time during 2014. On January 31, 2015, the Police Department asked the government legal office for an opinion on whether granting this request would violate the worshippers' right to freedom of religion. 4.____

   A. 2-4:G-1 B. 2-5:G1 C. 2-5:B-1 D. 2-4:B1

5. In 2014, a woman filed suit against the Board of Elections. She alleged that she had not been permitted to vote at her usual polling place in the 2013 election and had been told she was not registered there. She claimed that she had always voted there and that her record card had been lost. This was the fourth case of its type for this agency. 5.____

   A. 6-4:4 B. 6-3:C4 C. 3-4:6 D. 6-3:4

6. A lawsuit was brought in 2011 by the Ace Pinball Machine Company against the Commissioner of Consumer Affairs. The lawsuit contested an ordinance which banned the use of pinball machines on the ground that they are gambling devices. This was the third lawsuit to which the Department of Consumer Affairs was a party. 6.____

   A. 4-1:1 B. 4-3:F1 C. 4-1:3 D. 3F-4:1

7. You are instructed by your supervisor to type a statement that must be signed by the person making the statement and by three witnesses to the signature. The typed statement will take two pages and will leave no room for signatures if the normal margin is maintained at the bottom of the second page. 7.____
In this situation, the PREFERRED method is to type

A. the signature lines below the normal margin on the second page
B. nothing further and have the witnesses sign without a typed signature line
C. the signature lines on a third page
D. some of the text and the signature lines on a third page

8. Certain legal documents always begin with a statement of venue - that is, the county and state in which the document is executed. This is usually boxed with a parentheses or colons. 8.____
The one of the following documents that ALWAYS bears a statement of venue in a prominent position at its head is a(n)

A. affidavit
B. memorandum of law
C. contract of sale
D. will

9. A court stenographer is to take stenographic notes and transcribe the statements of a person under oath. The person has a heavy accent and speaks in ungrammatical and broken English. 9.____
When he or she is transcribing the testimony, of the following, the BEST thing for them to do is to

A. transcribe the testimony exactly as spoken, making no grammatical changes
B. make only the grammatical changes which would clarify the client's statements
C. make all grammatical changes so that the testimony is in standard English form
D. ask the client's permission before making any grammatical changes

10. When the material typed on a printed form does not fill the space provided, a Z-ruling is frequently drawn to fill up the unused space. 10.____
The MAIN purpose of this practice is to

A. make the document more pleasing to the eye
B. indicate that the preceding material is correct
C. insure that the document is not altered
D. show that the lawyer has read it

11. After you had typed an original and five copies of a certain document, some changes were made in ink on the original and were initialed by all the parties. The original was signed by all the parties, and the signatures were notarized. 11.____
Which of the following should *generally* be typed on the copies BEFORE filing the original and the copies? The inked changes

A. but not the signatures, initials, or notarial data
B. the signatures and the initials but not the notarial data
C. and the notarial data but not the signatures or initials
D. the signatures, the initials, and the notarial data

12. The first paragraph of a noncourt agreement *generally* contains all of the following EXCEPT the 12.____

 A. specific terms of the agreement
 B. date of the agreement
 C. purpose of the agreement
 D. names of the parties involved

13. When typing an answer in a court proceeding, the place where the word ANSWER should be typed on the first page of the document is 13.____

 A. at the upper left-hand corner
 B. below the index number and to the right of the box containing the names of the parties to the action
 C. above the index number and to the right of the box containing the names of the parties to the action
 D. to the left of the names of the attorneys for the defendant

14. Which one of the following statements BEST describes the legal document called an acknowledgment? 14.____
It is

 A. an answer to an affidavit
 B. a receipt issued by the court when a document is filed
 C. proof of service of a summons
 D. a declaration that a signature is valid

15. Suppose you typed the original and three copies of a legal document which was dictated by an attorney in your office. He has already signed the original copy, and corrections have been made on all copies. 15.____
Regarding the copies, which one of the following procedures is the PROPER one to follow?

 A. Leave the signature line blank on the copies
 B. Ask the attorney to sign the copies
 C. Print or type the attorney's name on the signature line on the copies
 D. Sign your name to the copies followed by the attorney's initials

16. Suppose your office is defending a particular person in a court action. This person comes to the office and asks to see some of the lawyer's working papers in his file. The lawyer assigned to the case is out of the office at the time. 16.____
You SHOULD

 A. permit him to examine his entire file as long as he does not remove any materials from it
 B. make an appointment for the caller to come back later when the lawyer will be there
 C. ask him what working papers he wants to see and show him only those papers
 D. tell him that he needs written permission from the lawyer in order to see any records

17. Suppose that you receive a phone call from an official who is annoyed about a letter from your office which she just received. The lawyer who dictated the letter is not in the office at the moment. 17.____
Of the following, the BEST action for you to take is to

A. explain that the lawyer is out but that you will ask the lawyer to return her call when he returns
B. take down all of the details of her complaint and tell her that you will get back to her with an explanation
C. refer to the proper file so that you can give her an explanation of the reasons for the letter over the phone
D. make an appointment for her to stop by the office to speak with the lawyer

18. Suppose that you have taken dictation for an interoffice memorandum. You are asked to prepare it for distribution to four lawyers in your department whose names are given to you. You will type an original and make four copies. Which one of the following is CORRECT with regard to the typing of the lawyers' names? 18.____
The names of all of the lawyers should appear

A. *only* on the original
B. on the original and each copy should have the name of one lawyer
C. on each of the copies but not on the original
D. on the original and on all of the copies

19. Regarding the correct typing of punctuation, the GENERALLY accepted practice is that there should be 19.____

A. two spaces after a semi-colon
B. one space before an apostrophe used in the body of a word
C. no space between parentheses and the matter enclosed
D. one space before and after a hyphen

20. Suppose you have just completed typing an original and two copies of a letter requesting information. The original is to be signed by a lawyer in your office. The first copy is for the files, and the second is to be used as a reminder to follow up. 20.____
The PROPER time to file the file copy of the letter is

A. after the letter has been signed and corrections have been made on the copies
B. before you take the letter to the lawyer for his signature
C. after a follow-up letter has been sent
D. after a response to the letter has been received

21. A secretary in a legal office has just typed a letter. She has typed the copy distribution notation on the copies to indicate *blind copy distribution*. This *blind copy* notation shows that 21.____

A. copies of the letter are being sent to persons that the addressee does not know
B. copies of the letter are being sent to other persons without the addressee's knowledge
C. a copy of the letter will be enlarged for a legally blind person
D. a copy of the letter is being given as an extra copy to the addressee

22. Suppose that one of the attorneys in your office dictates material to you without indicating punctuation. He has asked that you give him, as soon as possible, a single copy of a rough draft to be triple-spaced so that he can make corrections.
Of the following, what is the BEST thing for you to do in this situation? 22.____

A. Assume that no punctuation is desired in the material
B. Insert the punctuation as you type the rough draft
C. Transcribe the material exactly as dictated, but attach a note to the attorney stating your suggested changes
D. Before you start to type the draft, tell the attorney you want to read back your notes so that he can indicate punctuation

23. When it is necessary to type a mailing notation such as CERTIFIED, REGISTERED, or FEDEX on an envelope, the GENERALLY accepted place to type it is 23.____

A. directly above the address
B. in the area below where the stamp will be affixed
C. in the lower left-hand corner
D. in the upper left-hand corner

24. When taking a citation of a case in shorthand, which of the following should you write FIRST if you are having difficulty keeping up with the dictation? 24.____

A. Volume and page number
B. Title of volume
C. Name of plaintiff
D. Name of defendant

25. All of the following abbreviations and their meanings are correctly paired EXCEPT 25.____

A. viz. - namely
B. ibid. - refer
C. n.b. - note well
D. q.v. - which see

KEY (CORRECT ANSWERS)

1. D
2. D
3. B
4. B
5. A
6. C
7. D
8. A
9. A
10. C
11. D
12. A
13. B
14. D
15. C
16. B
17. A
18. D
19. C
20. A
21. B
22. B
23. B
24. A
25. B

EXAMINATION SECTION
TEST 1

DIRECTIONS: Each question or incomplete statement is followed by several suggested answers or completions. Select the one that BEST answers the question or completes the statement. *PRINT THE LETTER OF THE CORRECT ANSWER IN THE SPACE AT THE RIGHT.*

Questions 1-50.

DIRECTIONS: Each of Questions 1 through 50 consists of a word in capital letters followed by four suggested meanings of the word. For each question, choose the word or phrase which means MOST NEARLY the same as the word in capital letters.

1. ABUT 1.___
   A. abandon B. assist C. border on D. renounce

2. ABSCOND 2.___
   A. draw in B. give up
   C. refrain from D. deal off

3. BEQUEATH 3.___
   A. deaden B. hand down C. make sad D. scold

4. BOGUS 4.___
   A. sad B. false C. shocking D. stolen

5. CALAMITY 5.___
   A. disaster B. female C. insanity D. patriot

6. COMPULSORY 6.___
   A. binding B. ordinary C. protected D. ruling

7. CONSIGN 7.___
   A. agree with B. benefit
   C. commit D. drive down

8. DEBILITY 8.___
   A. failure B. legality
   C. quality D. weakness

9. DEFRAUD 9.___
   A. cheat B. deny
   C. reveal D. tie

10. DEPOSITION 10.___
    A. absence B. publication
    C. removal D. testimony

11. DOMICILE 11.___
    A. anger B. dwelling
    C. tame D. willing

12. HEARSAY 12.___
    A. selfish B. serious C. rumor D. unlikely

13. HOMOGENEOUS 13.___
    A. human B. racial C. similar D. unwise

14. ILLICIT 14.___
    A. understood B. uneven C. unkind D. unlawful

15. LEDGER 15.___
    A. book of accounts B. editor
    C. periodical D. shelf

16. NARRATIVE 16.___
    A. gossip B. natural C. negative D. story

17. PLAUSIBLE 17.___
    A. reasonable B. respectful C. responsible D. rightful

18. RECIPIENT 18.___
    A. absentee B. receiver C. speaker D. substitute

19. SUBSTANTIATE 19.___
    A. appear for B. arrange
    C. confirm D. combine

20. SURMISE 20.___
    A. aim B. break C. guess D. order

21. ALTER EGO 21.___
    A. business partner B. confidential friend
    C. guide D. subconscious conflict

22. FOURTH ESTATE 22.___
    A. the aristocracy B. the clergy
    C. the judiciary D. the newspapers

23. IMPEACH 23.___
    A. accuse B. find guilty
    C. remove D. try

24. PROPENSITY 24.___
    A. dislike B. helpfulness
    C. inclination D. supervision

25. SPLENETIC 25.___
    A. charming B. peevish C. shining D. sluggish

26. SUBORN 26.___
    A. bribe someone to commit perjury
    B. demote someone several levels in rank
    C. deride
    D. substitute

27. TALISMAN 27.___
   A. charm
   B. juror
   C. prayer shawl
   D. native

28. VITREOUS 28.___
   A. corroding
   B. glassy
   C. nourishing
   D. sticky

29. WRY 29.___
   A. comic
   B. grained
   C. resilient
   D. twisted

30. SIGNATORY 30.___
   A. lawyer who draws up a legal document
   B. document that must be signed by a judge
   C. person who signs a document
   D. true copy of a signature

31. RETAINER 31.___
   A. fee paid to a lawyer for his services
   B. document held by a third party
   C. court decision to send a prisoner back to custody pending trial
   D. legal requirement to keep certain types of files

32. BEQUEATH 32.___
   A. to receive assistance from a charitable organization
   B. to give personal property by will to another
   C. to transfer real property from one person to another
   D. to receive an inheritance upon the death of a relative

33. RATIFY 33.___
   A. approve and sanction
   B. forego
   C. produce evidence
   D. summarize

34. CODICIL 34.___
   A. document introduced in evidence in a civil action
   B. subsection of a law
   C. type of legal action that can be brought by a plaintiff
   D. supplement or an addition to a will

35. ALIAS 35.___
   A. assumed name
   B. in favor of
   C. against
   D. a writ

36. PROXY 36.___
   A. a phony document in a real estate transaction
   B. an opinion by a judge of a civil court
   C. a document containing appointment of an agent
   D. a summons in a lawsuit

37. ALLEGED 37.___
   A. innocent
   B. asserted
   C. guilty
   D. called upon

38. EXECUTE 38.___
    A. to complete a legal document by signing it
    B. to set requirements
    C. to render services to a duly elected executive of a municipality
    D. to initiate legal action such as a lawsuit

39. NOTARY PUBLIC 39.___
    A. lawyer who is running for public office
    B. judge who hears minor cases
    C. public officer, one of whose functions is to administer oaths
    D. lawyer who gives free legal services to persons unable to pay

40. WAIVE 40.___
    A. to disturb a calm state of affairs
    B. to knowingly renounce a right or claim
    C. to pardon someone for a minor fault
    D. to purposely mislead a person during an investigation

41. ARRAIGN 41.___
    A. to prevent an escape
    B. to defend a prisoner
    C. to verify a document
    D. to accuse in a court of law

42. VOLUNTARY 42.___
    A. by free choice
    B. necessary
    C. important
    D. by design

43. INJUNCTION 43.___
    A. act of prohibiting
    B. process of inserting
    C. means of arbitrating
    D. freedom of action

44. AMICABLE 44.___
    A. compelled
    B. friendly
    C. unimportant
    D. insignificant

45. CLOSED SHOP 45.___
    A. one that employs only members of a union
    B. one that employs union members and unaffiliated employees
    C. one that employs only employees with previous experience
    D. one that employs skilled and unskilled workers

46. ABDUCT 46.___
    A. lead B. kidnap C. sudden D. worthless

47. BIAS 47.___
    A. ability B. envy C. prejudice D. privilege

48. COERCE 48.___
    A. cancel B. force C. rescind D. rugged

49. CONDONE 49.___
A. combine B. pardon C. revive D. spice

50. CONSISTENCY 50.___
A. bravery B. readiness
C. strain D. uniformity

KEY (CORRECT ANSWERS)

1. C	11. B	21. B	31. A	41. D
2. D	12. C	22. D	32. B	42. A
3. B	13. C	23. A	33. A	43. A
4. B	14. D	24. C	34. D	44. B
5. A	15. A	25. B	35. A	45. A
6. A	16. D	26. A	36. C	46. B
7. C	17. A	27. A	37. B	47. C
8. D	18. B	28. B	38. A	48. B
9. A	19. C	29. D	39. C	49. B
10. D	20. C	30. C	40. B	50. D

TEST 2

DIRECTIONS: Each question or incomplete statement is followed by several suggested answers or completions. Select the one that BEST answers the question or completes the statement. *PRINT THE LETTER OF THE CORRECT ANSWER IN THE SPACE AT THE RIGHT.*

1. In the sentence, *The prisoner was fractious when brought to the station house*, the word *fractious* means MOST NEARLY 1.____
   A. penitent B. talkative
   C. irascible D. broken-hearted

2. In the sentence, *The judge was implacable when the attorney pleaded for leniency*, the word *implacable* means MOST NEARLY 2.____
   A. inexorable B. disinterested
   C. inattentive D. indifferent

3. In the sentence, *The court ordered the mendacious statements stricken from the record*, the word *mendacious* means MOST NEARLY 3.____
   A. begging B. lying
   C. threatening D. lengthy

4. In the sentence, *The district attorney spoke in a strident voice*, the word *strident* means MOST NEARLY 4.____
   A. loud B. harsh-sounding
   C. sing-song D. low

5. In the sentence, *The speaker had a predilection for long sentences*, the word *predilection* means MOST NEARLY 5.____
   A. aversion B. talent
   C. propensity D. diffidence

6. A person who has an uncontrollable desire to steal without need is called a 6.____
   A. dipsomaniac B. kleptomaniac
   C. monomaniac D. pyromaniac

7. In the sentence, *Malice was immanent in all his remarks*, the word *immanent* means MOST NEARLY 7.____
   A. elevated B. inherent
   C. threatening D. foreign

8. In the sentence, *The extant copies of the document were found in the safe*, the word *extant* means MOST NEARLY 8.____
   A. existing B. original
   C. forged D. duplicate

9. In the sentence, *The recruit was more complaisant after the captain spoke to him*, the word *complaisant* means MOST NEARLY 9.____
   A. calm B. affable
   C. irritable D. confident

10. In the sentence, *The man was captured under highly creditable circumstances*, the word *creditable* means MOST NEARLY 10.___

A. doubtful B. believable
C. praiseworthy D. unexpected

11. In the sentence, *His superior officers were more sagacious than he*, the word *sagacious* means MOST NEARLY 11.___

A. shrewd B. obtuse
C. absurd D. verbose

12. In the sentence, *He spoke with impunity*, the word *impunity* means MOST NEARLY 12.___

A. rashness B. caution
C. without fear D. immunity

13. In the sentence, *The new officer displayed unusual temerity during the emergency*, the word *temerity* means MOST NEARLY 13.___

A. fear B. rashness
C. calmness D. anxiety

14. In the sentence, *The portions of food were parsimoniously served*, the word *parsimoniously* means MOST NEARLY 14.___

A. stingily B. piously
C. elaborately D. generously

15. In the sentence, *Generally the speaker's remarks were sententious*, the word *sententious* means MOST NEARLY 15.___

A. verbose B. witty
C. argumentative D. pithy

Questions 16-20.

DIRECTIONS: Next to the number which corresponds with the number of each item in Column I, place the letter preceding the adjective in Column II which BEST describes the persons in Column I.

COLUMN I	COLUMN II	
16. Talkative woman	A. abstemious	16.___
17. Person on a reducing diet	B. pompous	17.___
18. Scholarly professor	C. erudite	18.___
19. Man who seldom speaks	D. benevolent	19.___
20. Charitable person	E. docile	20.___
	F. loquacious	
	G. indefatigable	
	H. taciturn	

Questions 21-25.

DIRECTIONS: Next to the number which corresponds with the number preceding each profession in Column I, place the letter preceding the word in Column II which BEST explains the subject matter of that profession.

COLUMN I	COLUMN II	
21. Geologist	A. animals	21.___
22. Oculist	B. eyes	22.___
23. Podiatrist	C. feet	23.___
24. Palmist	D. fortune-telling	24.___
25. Zoologist	E. language	25.___
	F. rocks	
	G. stamps	
	H. woman	

Questions 26-30.

DIRECTIONS: Next to the number corresponding to the number of each of the words in Column I, place the letter preceding the word in Column II that is MOST NEARLY OPPOSITE to it in meaning.

COLUMN I	COLUMN II	
26. comely	A. beautiful	26.___
27. eminent	B. cowardly	27.___
28. frugal	C. kind	28.___
29. gullible	D. sedate	29.___
30. valiant	E. shrewd	30.___
	F. ugly	
	G. unknown	
	H. wasteful	

KEY (CORRECT ANSWERS)

1.	C	11.	A	21.	F
2.	A	12.	D	22.	B
3.	B	13.	B	23.	C
4.	B	14.	A	24.	D
5.	C	15.	D	25.	A
6.	B	16.	F	26.	F
7.	B	17.	A	27.	G
8.	A	18.	C	28.	H
9.	B	19.	H	29.	E
10.	C	20.	D	30.	B

EXAMINATION SECTION
TEST 1

DIRECTIONS: Each question or incomplete statement is followed by several suggested answers or completions. Select the one that BEST answers the question or completes the statement. *PRINT THE LETTER OF THE CORRECT ANSWER IN THE SPACE AT THE RIGHT.*

Questions 1-25.

DIRECTIONS: In each of Questions 1 through 25, select the lettered word or phrase which means MOST NEARLY the same as the capitalized word.

1. INTERROGATE 1.___
   A. question B. arrest C. search D. rebuff

2. PERVERSE 2.___
   A. manageable
   B. poetic
   C. contrary
   D. patient

3. ADVOCATE 3.___
   A. champion
   B. employ
   C. select
   D. advise

4. APPARENT 4.___
   A. desirable
   B. clear
   C. partial
   D. possible

5. INSINUATE 5.___
   A. survey
   B. strengthen
   C. suggest
   D. insist

6. MOMENTOUS 6.___
   A. important B. immediate C. delayed D. short

7. AUXILIARY 7.___
   A. exciting B. assisting C. upsetting D. available

8. ADMONISH 8.___
   A. praise B. increase C. warn D. polish

9. ANTICIPATE 9.___
   A. agree B. expect C. conceal D. approve

10. APPREHEND 10.___
    A. confuse B. sentence C. release D. seize

11. CLEMENCY 11.___
    A. silence B. freedom C. mercy D. severity

12. THWART 12.___
    A. enrage B. strike C. choke D. block

13. RELINQUISH 13.___
    A. stretch B. give up C. weaken D. flee from
14. CURTAIL 14.___
    A. stop B. reduce C. repair D. insult
15. INACCESSIBLE 15.___
    A. obstinate B. unreachable
    C. unreasonable D. puzzling
16. PERTINENT 16.___
    A. related B. saucy C. durable D. impatient
17. INTIMIDATE 17.___
    A. encourage B. hunt C. beat D. frighten
18. INTEGRITY 18.___
    A. honesty B. wisdom
    C. understanding D. persistence
19. UTILIZE 19.___
    A. use B. manufacture
    C. help D. include
20. SUPPLEMENT 20.___
    A. regulate B. demand C. add D. answer
21. INDISPENSABLE 21.___
    A. essential B. neglected
    C. truthful D. unnecessary
22. ATTAIN 22.___
    A. introduce B. spoil C. achieve D. study
23. PRECEDE 23.___
    A. break away B. go ahead
    C. begin D. come before
24. HAZARD 24.___
    A. penalty B. adventure C. handicap D. danger
25. DETRIMENTAL 25.___
    A. uncertain B. harmful C. fierce D. horrible

KEY (CORRECT ANSWERS)

1. A	6. A	11. C	16. A	21. A
2. C	7. B	12. D	17. D	22. C
3. A	8. C	13. B	18. A	23. D
4. B	9. B	14. B	19. A	24. D
5. C	10. D	15. B	20. C	25. B

TEST 2

DIRECTIONS: Each question or incomplete statement is followed by several suggested answers or completions. Select the one that BEST answers the question or completes the statement. *PRINT THE LETTER OF THE CORRECT ANSWER IN THE SPACE AT THE RIGHT.*

Questions 1-20.

DIRECTIONS: In each of Questions 1 through 20, select the lettered word or phrase which means MOST NEARLY the same as the capitalized word.

1. IMPLY 1.___
   A. agree to B. hint at C. laugh at
   D. mimic E. reduce

2. APPRAISAL 2.___
   A. allowance B. composition C. prohibition
   D. quantity E. valuation

3. DISBURSE 3.___
   A. approve B. expend C. prevent
   D. relay E. restrict

4. POSTERITY 4.___
   A. back payment B. current procedure C. final effort
   D. future generations E. rare specimen

5. PUNCTUAL 5.___
   A. clear B. honest C. polite
   D. prompt E. prudent

6. PRECARIOUS 6.___
   A. abundant B. alarmed C. cautious
   D. insecure E. placid

7. FOSTER 7.___
   A. delegate B. demote C. encourage
   D. plead E. surround

8. PINNACLE 8.___
   A. center B. crisis C. outcome
   D. peak E. personification

9. COMPONENT 9.___
   A. flattery B. opposite C. part
   D. revision E. trend

10. SOLICIT 10.___
   A. ask B. prohibit C. promise
   D. revoke E. surprise

11. LIAISON 11.___
   A. asset B. coordination C. difference
   D. policy E. procedure

12. ALLEGE 12.___
   A. assert B. break C. irritate
   D. reduce E. wait

13. INFILTRATION 13.___
   A. consumption B. disposal C. enforcement
   D. penetration E. seizure

14. SALVAGE 14.___
   A. announce B. combine C. prolong
   D. save E. try

15. MOTIVE 15.___
   A. attack B. favor C. incentive
   D. patience E. tribute

16. PROVOKE 16.___
   A. adjust B. incite C. leave
   D. obtain E. practice

17. SURGE 17.___
   A. branch B. contract C. revenge
   D. rush E. want

18. MAGNIFY 18.___
   A. attract B. demand C. generate
   D. increase E. puzzle

19. PREPONDERANCE 19.___
   A. decision B. judgment C. outweighing
   D. submission E. warning

20. ABATE 20.___
   A. assist B. coerce C. diminish
   D. indulge E. trade

Questions 21-30.

DIRECTIONS: In each of Questions 21 through 30, select the lettered word or phrase which means MOST NEARLY, the same as, or the opposite of, the capitalized word.

21. VINDICTIVE 21.___
   A. centrifugal B. forgiving C. molten
   D. tedious E. vivacious

22. SCOPE 22.___
   A. compact B. detriment C. facsimile
   D. potable E. range

23. HINDER 23.___
    A. amplify B. aver C. method
    D. observe E. retard

24. IRATE 24.___
    A. adhere B. angry C. authentic
    D. peremptory E. vacillate

25. APATHY 25.___
    A. accessory B. availability C. fervor
    D. pacify E. stride

26. LUCRATIVE 26.___
    A. effective B. imperfect C. injurious
    D. timely E. worthless

27. DIVERSITY 27.___
    A. convection B. slip C. temerity
    D. uniformity E. viscosity

28. OVERT 28.___
    A. laugh B. lighter C. orifice
    D. quay E. sly

29. SPORADIC 29.___
    A. divide B. incumbrance C. livid
    D. occasional E. original

30. PREVARICATE 30.___
    A. hesitate B. increase C. lie
    D. procrastinate E. reject

KEY (CORRECT ANSWERS)

1.	B	11.	B	21.	B
2.	E	12.	A	22.	E
3.	B	13.	D	23.	E
4.	D	14.	D	24.	B
5.	D	15.	C	25.	C
6.	D	16.	B	26.	E
7.	C	17.	D	27.	D
8.	D	18.	D	28.	E
9.	C	19.	C	29.	D
10.	A	20.	C	30.	C

TEST 3

DIRECTIONS: Each question or incomplete statement is followed by several suggested answers or completions. Select the one that BEST answers the question or completes the statement. *PRINT THE LETTER OF THE CORRECT ANSWER IN THE SPACE AT THE RIGHT.*

Questions 1-30.

DIRECTIONS: In each of Questions 1 through 30, select the lettered word which means MOST NEARLY the same as the capitalized word.

1. AVARICE 1.____
   A. flight B. greed C. pride D. thrift
2. PREDATORY 2.____
   A. offensive B. plundering
   C. previous D. timeless
3. VINDICATE 3.____
   A. clear B. conquer C. correct D. illustrate
4. INVETERATE 4.____
   A. backward B. erect C. habitual D. lucky
5. DISCERN 5.____
   A. describe B. fabricate C. recognize D. seek
6. COMPLACENT 6.____
   A. indulgent B. listless C. overjoyed D. satisfied
7. ILLICIT 7.____
   A. insecure B. unclear C. unlawful D. unlimited
8. PROCRASTINATE 8.____
   A. declare B. multiply C. postpone D. steal
9. IMPASSIVE 9.____
   A. calm B. frustrated
   C. thoughtful D. unhappy
10. AMICABLE 10.____
    A. cheerful B. flexible
    C. friendly D. poised
11. FEASIBLE 11.____
    A. breakable B. easy
    C. likeable D. practicable
12. INNOCUOUS 12.____
    A. harmless B. insecure
    C. insincere D. unfavorable

13. OSTENSIBLE 13.___
A. apparent B. hesitant C. reluctant D. showy

14. INDOMITABLE 14.___
A. excessive B. unconquerable
C. unreasonable D. unthinkable

15. CRAVEN 15.___
A. cowardly B. hidden C. miserly D. needed

16. ALLAY 16.___
A. discuss B. quiet C. refine D. remove

17. ALLUDE 17.___
A. denounce B. refer C. state D. support

18. NEGLIGENCE 18.___
A. carelessness B. denial
C. objection D. refusal

19. AMEND 19.___
A. correct B. destroy C. end D. list

20. RELEVANT 20.___
A. conclusive B. careful
C. obvious D. related

21. VERIFY 21.___
A. challenge B. change C. confirm D. reveal

22. INSIGNIFICANT 22.___
A. incorrect B. limited
C. unimportant D. undesirable

23. RESCIND 23.___
A. annul B. deride C. extol D. indulge

24. AUGMENT 24.___
A. alter B. increase C. obey D. perceive

25. AUTONOMOUS 25.___
A. conceptual B. constant
C. defamatory D. independent

26. TRANSCRIPT 26.___
A. copy B. report C. sentence D. termination

27. DISCORDANT 27.___
A. quarrelsome B. comprised
C. effusive D. harmonious

28. DISTEND 28.___
A. constrict B. dilate C. redeem D. silence

29. EMANATE 29.___
    A. bridge B. coherency C. conquer D. flow

30. EXULTANT 30.___
    A. easily upset
    B. in high spirits
    C. subject to moods
    D. very much over-priced

KEY (CORRECT ANSWERS)

1.	B	11.	D	21.	C
2.	B	12.	A	22.	C
3.	A	13.	A	23.	A
4.	C	14.	B	24.	B
5.	C	15.	A	25.	D
6.	D	16.	B	26.	A
7.	C	17.	B	27.	A
8.	C	18.	A	28.	B
9.	A	19.	A	29.	D
10.	C	20.	D	30.	B

READING COMPREHENSION
UNDERSTANDING AND INTERPRETING WRITTEN MATERIAL

EXAMINATION SECTION
TEST 1

DIRECTIONS: Each question or incomplete statement is followed by several suggested answers or completions. Select the one that BEST answers the question or completes the statement. *PRINT THE LETTER OF THE CORRECT ANSWER IN THE SPACE AT THE RIGHT.*

Questions 1-6.

DIRECTIONS: Questions 1 through 6 are to be answered SOLELY on the basis of the following passage.

Delinquency and crime and reactions to them are social products and are socially defined. Society as a whole, not individuals, creates and defines rules, pejoratively labels those who break rules, and prescribes ways for reacting to the labeled person. Moreover, at times the societal process of defining, labeling, and reacting may not affect behavior but at other times it is influential in determining both who shall enter the correctional process and what its outcome will be

What's more, the labeling process is often a means of isolating offenders from, rather than integrating them in, effective participation in such major societal institutions as schools, businesses, unions, and political, community, and fraternal organizations. These institutions are the major access routes to a successful, non-delinquent career. Those who are in power in them are the gatekeepers of society and, if offenders and correctional programs are isolated from them, then the personal wishes and characteristics of offenders will have little bearing on whether correctional programs succeed or fail.

1. According to the above passage, the MAJOR determinant of whether an offender will succeed in society is his 1.____

   A. self-confidence and general intelligence
   B. degree of participation in the major societal institutions
   C. attitude toward the entire criminal justice system
   D. overall criminal record

2. The above passage suggests that the isolation of offenders from certain groups within society through the labeling process is 2.____

   A. intentional
   B. unlawful
   C. beneficial
   D. irreversible

3. Of the following, the MOST appropriate title for the passage is 3.____

   A. METHODS OF REFORMING THE ATTITUDES OF SOCIETY
   B. UNJUST JUSTICE
   C. DELINQUENCY AND CRIME
   D. SOCIETY'S REJECTION OF OFFENDERS

4. According to the passage, delinquency and crime are created by the 4.____

   A. characteristics of offenders
   B. correctional process itself
   C. operations of society
   D. gatekeepers of major institutions

5. Of the following suggested methods of helping offenders adjust to society, the one which the passage would be LEAST likely to favor would be to 5.____

   A. establish cooperative relations between correctional programs in cooperation with influential members of society
   B. keep the public informed of current developments in the corrections field by contributing information to local newspapers
   C. create an organizational structure within correctional institutions which, wherever practicable, resembles life in society
   D. encourage offenders to maintain close ties with other offenders with whom they become friendly while incarcerated

6. According to the passage, the rehabilitation of the offender is MOST likely to be determined by 6.____

   A. the individual inmate himself
   B. dynamic reformation programs
   C. society as a whole
   D. the specific correctional institution

Questions 7-10.

DIRECTIONS: Questions 7 through 10 are to be answered SOLELY on the basis of the following paragraph.

Urban crime rates are generally higher than those prevailing in rural areas. This apparent preponderance of urban crime has been observed by many criminologists both here and abroad and, although the factual basis for their conclusion that more crime occurs in urban areas does not lend itself to close measurement, there seems to be sufficient reason to accept it at face value. But there is an increasing body of evidence accumulating in the United States indicative that a profound change in these relationships may be in progress. For murder and rape, the rural crime rate of this country now equals the urban rate. As to all homicides, it exceeds the urban crime rate of the New England, Middle Atlantic, and North Central states, and shows such impressive advances for aggravated assault and robbery as to greatly reduce the former disparity. Such changes raise the question whether rural crimes, reacting to new means of transport and consequent interchange of population, which are urban influences, may not now be in the process of attaining urban crime levels. Certain it is that crimes against the person have for centuries been relatively more numerous in rural areas than crimes against property. Hence, the new trend is in a sense an extension of a condition of long standing.

7. According to the above passage, the statement that crime rates are generally higher in urban areas than in rural areas 7.____

A. has not been definitely established although there is strong evidence to support such a view
B. is justified but does not necessarily indicate that more crime is actually committed in urban areas
C. has been definitely established despite some contrary evidence submitted by criminologists
D. is not justified since the facts gathered by many criminologists do not lend themselves to close measurement

8. Concerning the present relationship between rural and urban crime rates, it would be MOST correct to state, according to the above passage, that for 8.____

A. aggravated assault and robbery, the urban rate remained stationary while the rural rate increased
B. murder and rape, the rural rate equals the urban rate in the Middle Atlantic states
C. aggravated assault and robbery, the rural rate was formerly lower than the urban rate
D. murder and rape, the urban rate is less than the rural rate in the North Central states

9. The development of new means of transport, according to the above passage, 9.____

A. may or may not be an urban influence but it definitely contributed to a rise in rural crime levels
B. is an urban influence and may or may not contribute to a rise in rural crime levels
C. may or may not be an urban influence and may or may not contribute to a rise in rural crime levels
D. is an urban influence and has definitely contributed to a rise in rural crime levels

10. The new trend is BEST defined, according to the above passage, as a tendency for crimes against 10.____

A. the person to be more numerous in rural areas than they have been in the past in urban areas
B. property to be less numerous in urban areas than they are in rural areas
C. the person to be more numerous in rural areas than they have been in the past in rural areas
D. property to be more numerous in urban areas than they have been in the past in urban areas

Questions 11-15.

DIRECTIONS: Questions 11 through 15 are to be answered SOLELY on the basis of the following paragraph.

If we are to study crime in its widest social setting, we will find a variety of conduct which, although criminal in the legal sense, is not offensive to the moral conscience of a considerable number of persons. Traffic violations, for example, do not brand the offender as guilty of moral offense. In fact, the recipient of a traffic ticket is usually simply the subject of some good-natured joking by his friends. Although there may be indignation among certain groups of citizens against gambling and liquor law violations, these activities are often tolerated, if not openly supported, by the more numerous residents of the community. Indeed, certain social and service clubs regularly conduct gambling games and lotteries for the purpose of raising funds. Some communities regard violations involving the sale of liquor with little concern in order to profit from increased license fees and taxes paid by dealers. The thousand and one forms of political graft and corruption which infest our urban centers only occasionally arouse public condemnation and official action.

11. According to the above paragraph, all types of illegal conduct are 11.____

   A. condemned by all elements of the community
   B. considered a moral offense, although some are tolerated by a few citizens
   C. violations of the law, but some are acceptable to certain elements of the community
   D. found in a social setting which is not punishable by law

12. According to the above paragraph, traffic violations are GENERALLY considered by society as 12.____

   A. crimes requiring the maximum penalty set by the law
   B. more serious than violations of the liquor laws
   C. offenses against the morals of the community
   D. relatively minor offenses requiring minimum punishment

13. According to the above paragraph, a lottery conducted for the purpose of raising funds for a church 13.____

   A. is considered a serious violation of law
   B. may be tolerated by a community which has laws against gambling
   C. may be conducted under special laws demanded by the more numerous residents of a community
   D. arouses indignation in most communities

14. On the basis of the paragraph, the MOST likely reaction in the community to a police raid on a gambling casino would be 14.____

   A. more an attitude of indifference than interest in the raid
   B. general approval of the raid
   C. condemnation of the raid by most people
   D. demand for further action, since this raid is not sufficient to end gambling activities

15. The one of the following which BEST describes the central thought of this paragraph and would be MOST suitable as a title for it is 15.____

   A. CRIME AND THE POLICE
   B. PUBLIC CONDEMNATION OF GRAFT AND CORRUPTION
   C. GAMBLING IS NOT ALWAYS A VICIOUS BUSINESS
   D. PUBLIC ATTITUDE TOWARD LAW VIOLATIONS

Questions 16-18.

DIRECTIONS: Questions 16 through 18 are to be answered SOLELY on the basis of the following paragraphs.

The rise of urban-industrial society has complicated the social arrangements needed to regulate contacts between people. As a consequence, there has been an unprecedented increase in the volume of laws and regulations designed to control individual conduct and to govern the relationship of the individual to others. In a century there has been an eight-fold increase in the crimes for which one may be prosecuted.

For these offenses, the courts have the ultimate responsibility for redressing wrongs and convicting the guilty. The body of legal precepts gives the impression of an abstract and even-handed dispensation of justice. Actually, the personnel of the agencies applying these precepts are faced with the difficulties of fitting abstract principles to highly variable situations emerging from the dynamics of everyday life. It is inevitable that discrepancies should exist between precept and practice.

The legal institutions serve as a framework for the social order by their slowness to respond to the caprices of transitory fad. This valuable contribution exacts a price in terms of the inflexibility of legal institutions in responding to new circumstances. This possibility is promoted by the changes in values and norms of the dynamic larger culture of which the legal precepts are a part.

16. According to the above passage, the increase in the number of laws and regulations during the twentieth century can be attributed to the 16.____

A. complexity of modern industrial society
B. increased seriousness of offenses committed
C. growth of individualism
D. anonymity of urban living

17. According to the above passage, which of the following presents a problem to the staff of legal agencies? 17.____

A. The need to eliminate the discrepancy between precept and practice
B. The necessity to apply abstract legal precepts to rapidly changing conditions
C. The responsibility for reducing the number of abstract legal principles
D. The responsibility for understanding offenses in terms of the real life situations from which they emerge

18. According to the above passage, it can be concluded that legal institutions affect social institutions by 18.____

A. preventing change
B. keeping pace with its norms and values
C. changing its norms and values
D. providing stability

Questions 19-21.

DIRECTIONS: Questions 19 through 21 are to be answered SOLELY on the basis of the following paragraph.

This research lends additional emphasis to the contention that crime, as reported and recorded in the United States, is largely a function of social and cultural factors rather than biological, psychological, or entirely chance of factors. In the absence of significant biological variations or significant differences in basic mental processes on a regional or sectional basis, all other things being equal, one would expect a rather even crime rate from state to state. Since vast differences in crime rates on a sectional basis are found to persist over a period of time, one may hypothesize that subcultural variations of a regional or sectional nature are responsible for these regional or sectional patterns of crime. Even if this hypothesis cannot be accepted due to underreporting of crime, the least that the data may be said to demonstrate is a distinctly sectional variation in reporting and recording practices, indicating great disparities in sectional reactions to various types of human, or more specifically, criminal behavior.

19. According to the above paragraph, sectional crime rates 19.____

A. are not affected significantly by entirely chance factors in the absence of psychological factors
B. can be affected by biological variations or differences in basic mental processes
C. vary little with significant biological factors in the population
D. vary significantly in the absence of variable social and cultural factors

20. According to the above paragraph, great differences in the crime pattern and incidence in different sections of the United States may be said to be, assuming adequate reporting, 20.____

A. a function of sectional variations in reporting and recording practices
B. based on the specificity of some types of criminal behavior and the lack of a pattern in others
C. based primarily on differences in the extent of urbanization of the population
D. the result of regional cultural variations that are persistent over a period of time

21. According to the above paragraph, the statement that is MOST acceptable concerning the interpretation of crime data distribution by states or regions is that 21.____

A. a more or less even crime rate from state to state indicates absence of significant biological variations
B. consistent patterns of crime incidence are solely attributable to similar cultural and social factors
C. failure to report crime that has occurred is indicative of differences in reaction to different types of crimes committed
D. uniform reporting practices tend to eliminate sectional disparities in causality of crime

Questions 22-26.

DIRECTIONS: Questions 22 through 26 are to be answered SOLELY on the basis of the following paragraph.

Criminals were once considered sinners who chose to offend against the laws of God and man. They were severely punished for their crimes. Modern criminologists regard society itself as in large part responsible for the crimes committed against it. Poverty, poor living conditions, and inadequate education are all causes of crime. Crime is fundamentally the result of society's failure to provide a decent life for all the people. It is especially common in times when values are changing, as after a war, or in countries where people of different backgrounds and values are thrown together, as in the United States. Crimes, generally speaking, are fewer in countries where there is a settled way of life and a traditional respect for law.

22. This passage deals with 22.____

A. criminals
B. society
C. the reasons for crime
D. crime in the United States

23. The MAIN idea of this passage is that 23.____

A. crime is common when values are changing
B. crime is the result of poverty
C. traditional respect for law prevents a crime
D. society is largely responsible for crime

24. According to the passage, which is NOT a cause of crime? 24.____

A. Poverty
B. Wickedness
C. Ethnic mixing
D. Unsettled way of life

25. Crime is MOST common in 25.____

A. periods of instability
B. the United States
C. wartime
D. suburbs

26. To prevent crime, the author implies that society should 26.____

A. provide stiffer penalties for criminals
B. provide a decent way of life for everyone
C. segregate the poor
D. give broader powers to the police

Questions 27-30.

DIRECTIONS: Questions 27 through 30 are to be answered SOLELY on the basis of the following passage.

Perpetrators of crimes are often described by witnesses or victims in terms of salient facial features. The Bertillon System of identification which preceded the widespread use of fingerprints was based on body measurements. Recently, there have been developments in the quantification of procedures used in the classification and comparison of facial characteristics. Devices are now available which enable a trained operator, with the aid of a witness, to form a composite picture of a suspect's face and to translate that composite into a numerical code. Further developments in this area are possible, using computers to develop efficient sequences of questions so that witnesses may quickly arrive at the proper description.

Recent studies of voice analysis and synthesis, originally motivated by problems of efficient telephone transmission, have led to the development of the audio-frequency profile or *voice print*. Each voice print may be sufficiently unique to permit development of a classification system that will make possible positive identification of the source of a voice print. This method of identification, using an expert to identify the voice patterns, has been introduced in more than 40 cases by 15 different police departments. As with all identification systems that rely on experts to perform the identification, controlled laboratory tests are needed to establish with care the relative frequency of errors of omission and commission made by experts.

27. The MOST appropriate title for the above passage is 27.____

    A. TECHNOLOGY IN MODERN INVESTIGATIVE DETECTION
    B. IDENTIFICATION BY PHYSICAL FEATURES
    C. VERIFICATION OF IDENTIFICATIONS BY EXPERTS
    D. THE USE OF ELECTRONIC IDENTIFICATION TECHNIQUES

28. According to the above passage, computers may be used in conjunction with which of the following identification techniques? 28.____

    A. Fingerprints
    B. Bertillon System
    C. Voice prints
    D. Composite Facial Pictures

29. According to the above passage, the ability to identify individuals based on facial characteristics has improved as a result of 29.____

    A. an increase in the number of facial types which can be shown to witnesses
    B. information which is derived from other body measurements
    C. coded classification and comparison techniques
    D. greater reliance upon experts to make the identifications

30. According to the above passage, it is CORRECT to state that audio-frequency profiles or *voice prints* 30.____

    A. have been decisive in many prosecutions
    B. reduce the number of errors made by experts
    C. developed as a result of problems in telephonic communications
    D. are unlikely to result in positive identifications

KEY (CORRECT ANSWERS)

1.	B	16.	A
2.	A	17.	B
3.	D	18.	D
4.	C	19.	D
5.	D	20.	D
6.	C	21.	C
7.	B	22.	C
8.	C	23.	A
9.	D	24.	B
10.	C	25.	A
11.	C	26.	B
12.	D	27.	B
13.	B	28.	D
14.	A	29.	C
15.	D	30.	C

TEST 2

DIRECTIONS: Each question or incomplete statement is followed by several suggested answers or completions. Select the one that BEST answers the question or completes the statement. *PRINT THE LETTER OF THE CORRECT ANSWER IN THE SPACE AT THE RIGHT.*

Questions 1-7.

DIRECTIONS: Questions 1 through 7 are to be answered SOLELY on the basis of the following rules. These rules are not intended to be an exact copy of the rules of any institution.

SECTION OF RULES

All members of the department shall treat as confidential the official business of the department. An employee shall under no circumstances impart information to anyone relating to the official business of the department, except when she is a witness under oath in a court of law. When answering a department telephone, an employee shall give the name of the institution to which she is attached, her rank, and full name. Officers shall not give the name of any bondsman or attorney to inmates. The head of the institution shall be notified immediately when an inmate requests an officer for the name of a bondsman or attorney. All inmates awaiting trial shall be advised that they are entitled to one free twenty-five cent telephone call-within the city. All other telephone calls must be paid for by the inmate. Officers assigned to the examination of parcels or letters for inmates shall do so with utmost care. Failure to discover contraband shall be presumptive evidence of negligence. When an officer is assigned to accompany an inmate to court, to the District Attorney's office, or elsewhere, she must handcuff the inmate and must, under no circumstances, visit any places except such as are designated in the document calling for the inmate's presence.

1. Assume that Mary Jones is assigned to the House of Detention as a Correction Officer with shield number 781. 1.____
When she answers the institution's phone, she should say

   A. House of Detention, Officer Mary Jones
   B. House of Detention, Officer Mary Jones, shield number 781
   C. Officer Mary Jones, shield number 781
   D. This is the House of Detention, Officer Jones speaking

2. An inmate awaiting trial asks for permission to make a telephone call to New Jersey. 2.____
She should be

   A. allowed to make the call if she has not made any other free calls
   B. permitted to make the call at her own expense
   C. told that only local telephone calls are permitted
   D. told that she will have to pay all charges over twenty-five cents

3. An inmate awaiting trial asks you for the name of a lawyer who will not charge a large fee, as she does not have much money. 3.____
You should

A. bring her request to the attention of the head of the institution
B. remind her that under the rules inmates are forbidden to ask an officer for the name of an attorney
C. tell her that you don't know any lawyers who charge low fees
D. tell her the state will furnish a lawyer without charge

4. A supervisor has an inmate whose case received a great deal of publicity in the newspapers. One day a reporter comes to the supervisor's home to interview him about this prisoner. 4.____
The supervisor should

A. give him only such information as has already appeared in the daily press
B. give him only such information which is not considered confidential
C. tell him that he is prohibited by the rules from discussing the case with him
D. tell him that an interview will be granted if he can produce a letter from the Commissioner giving him permission for the interview

5. An officer is assigned to deliver a prisoner to the hospital prison ward in accordance with a court order. He is given a department car and chauffeur for this purpose. Before he leaves, the Superintendent of the prison also gives him some important official papers requiring the Commissioner's immediate attention for delivery to Central Office. On the way to the hospital, he will pass Central Office. 5.____
He should stop at Central Office

A. and send the chauffeur in with the papers while he waits in the car with the prisoner
B. on his way back from the hospital, after he has delivered his prisoner
C. to deliver the papers, leaving the handcuffed prisoner in the car in charge of the chauffeur
D. to deliver the papers, taking the handcuffed prisoner with him

6. According to the rules, if an article of contraband is successfully smuggled into the prison in a package for an inmate, it is 6.____

A. possible that the contraband may have been extremely well concealed
B. possible that the employee who inspected the package did not realize that the article in question constituted contraband
C. probable that the employee who inspected the package was careless
D. sufficient cause to make the employee who inspected the package subject to dismissal

7. According to the rules, 7.____

A. an employee may testify about official business in court
B. only a competent court or the District Attorney can order a prisoner to be produced
C. sentenced inmates are not allowed to make telephone calls out of the Institution
D. while packages for inmates are censored, their personal mail is not

Questions 8-11.

DIRECTIONS: Questions 8 through 11 are to be answered on the basis of the following passage.

Female criminality is very much under-reported, especially if one considers offenses such as shoplifting, thefts by prostitutes, offenses against children, and homicide. There are even certain offenses such as homosexuality and exhibitionism that go practically unprosecuted if committed by women. Female offenders are really protected by men, even by victims, who are usually disinclined to complain to authorities. Since women play much less active roles in society than men do, one must be prepared for the fact that women are often the instigators of crimes committed by men and, as instigators, they are hard to detect. There are several crimes that are ordinarily highly detectable in men but have very low detectability in women. Her roles as homemaker, mother, nurse, wife, and so forth, permit the female to commit a crime and yet screen that crime from public view - for example, slowly poisoning her husband or treating her children abusively. In addition, law enforcement officers, judges, and juries are much more lenient toward women than toward men. Such considerations lead to the conclusion that criminality of women is *largely masked criminality.* Consequently, official statistics and records of criminality should be expected to under-report female offenses. The true measure of female crime must be sought from unofficial sources. The masked character of female crime and its gross under-reporting are consistent with the official view that the female is a very low risk for crime.

8. What has the writer inferred about the incidence of female offenses? 8.____

    A. It gives an adequate representation of the number of crimes committed by men but instigated by women.
    B. It is not to be considered an important area of criminality.
    C. It is understated because the classic female role makes her less visible to social scrutiny.
    D. In every crime the incidence of male offenses is more difficult to detect than that of women.

9. Judges are inclined to be lenient toward female offenders because 9.____

    A. the role of the woman in society has stereotyped her as maternal and non-hostile
    B. the majority of their crimes does not physically harm others
    C. they commit crimes which are difficult to detect
    D. official statistics report them as less likely to commit crimes

10. Of the following, the title MOST suitable for this passage is 10.____

    A. MALE CRIMINALITY
    B. THE PETTY OFFENDER
    C. THE FEMALE MURDERER
    D. EXPOSING FEMALE CRIMINALITY

11. According to the passage, which of the following crimes is LEAST likely to be prosecuted against a woman? 11.____

    A. Child abuse
    B. Exhibitionism
    C. Homicide
    D. Prostitution

Questions 12-16.

DIRECTIONS: Questions 12 through 16 are to be answered SOLELY on the basis of the following paragraph. Each of the questions consists of two statements. Read the paragraph carefully, and then mark your answer

A - if both statements are correct according to the information given in the paragraph
B - if both statements are incorrect according to the information given in the paragraph
C - if one statement is correct and one is incorrect according to the information given in the paragraph
D - if the correctness or incorrectness of one or both of the statements cannot be determined from the information given in the paragraph.

The twentieth century has opened to women many pursuits from which they were formerly excluded and thus has given them new opportunities for crime. Can we assume that as a result of this development female crime will change its nature and become like masculine crime through losing its masked character? In periods of pronounced social stress, such as war, in which women assume many roles otherwise open only to men, experience indicates that crimes of women against property increase. Can we assume, further, that simultaneously the amount of undiscovered female crime decreases? Further study contradicts the validity of this assumption. Their new roles have become wage earners and household heads, but they have not stopped being the homemakers, the rearers of children, the nurses, or the shoppers. With the burden of their social functions increased, their opportunities for crime have not undergone a process of substitution so much as a process of increase.

12. I. As women assumed increased social burdens, there was a marked change in the character of their opportunities for crime. 12.____
II. Although the crimes committed by women have increased, they are still fewer in number than those committed by men.

13. I. Male crime is less masked in character than female crime. 13.____
II. The opportunities of women to commit crimes have increased in the last fifty years.

14. I. In wartime, when they have increased employment opportunities, women commit fewer crimes against property. 14.____
II. When the social equality of women increases, the number of undetected crimes which they commit decreases.

15. I. In the period between 1900 and 1968, women did not gain many new opportunities for employment. 15.____
II. In a family unit, the role of the shopper is traditionally that of the wife rather than that of the husband.

16. I. The crime rate increases in periods of social stress, such as war. 16.____
II. Because women have not wanted to be limited to their traditional roles of homemaker and rearer of children, they have sought social equality with men.

Questions 17-18.

DIRECTIONS: Questions 17 and 18 are to be answered SOLELY on the basis of the following passage.

The public has become increasingly aware that rehabilitation that great battle cry of prison reform is one of the great myths of 20th century penology. The hard truth is that punishment and retribution are the primary, if not the only, functions served by most correctional institutions. Courts can provide enlightened rule-making to assist prison reform and ombudsmen can give prisoners a forum to consider their complaints but the results would be limited. The corrections system will never run with any real efficiency until: (a) prisoners want to be reformed; (b) prison administrators want to help them reform; (c) courts want to help both toward a system of reform; and (d) they all define reform in the same way. If this is not done, the criminal justice system will continue to operate on the model of concentric layers of coercion, a grossly inefficient model.

17. According to the above passage, all of the following will be required in order to improve the corrections system EXCEPT 17.____

    A. commitment to reform by prison administrators
    B. development by penal experts of criteria for meaningful rehabilitation
    C. acceptance by prisoners of the need for their cooperation
    D. assistance by the courts in providing a system where reform is possible

18. According to the above selection, meaningful prison reform is MOST likely to result from 18.____

    A. the appointment of ombudsmen to replace the courts in ruling on prisoners' complaints
    B. coordination by sociologists of efforts to improve prison conditions
    C. a realization by society that rehabilitation of prisoners is no longer a realistic objective
    D. the joint efforts of those directly concerned and a common understanding of the goals to be achieved

Questions 19-25.

DIRECTIONS: Each of Questions 19 through 25 begins with a statement. Your answer to each of these questions MUST be based only upon this statement and not on any other information you may have.

19. At any given moment, the number of people coming out of prisons in the United States is substantially as great as the number entering them. 19.____
Of the following, the MOST reasonable assumption on the basis of the preceding statement is that

    A. most prisoners in the United States prisons are recidivists
    B. the crime rate in this country is decreasing
    C. the crime rate in this country is increasing
    D. the prison population of this country is constant

20. The indeterminate sentence usually sets a lower limit for the time to be served, and an upper limit. In some cases, there is a maximum limit, but no minimum; in some, a minimum but no maximum; and in others, neither a maximum nor a minimum, the time to be served being determined by the prisoner's conduct and other considerations. In the preceding statement, the one of the following which is NOT given as a characteristic of the indeterminate sentence is that 20.____

A. sometimes the maximum time which must be served is not set at the time of sentence
B. sometimes the minimum time which must be served is not set at the time of sentence
C. the exact length of time to be served is fixed at the time of sentence
D. the length of time to be served may vary with the prisoner's behavior

21. Overcrowding in a prison makes segregation of prisoners more difficult, complicates the maintenance of order and discipline, and endangers health and morals. Of the following, the MOST reasonable assumption based on the preceding statement is that 21.____

A. if prisoners are allowed to associate too freely their health and morals will be endangered
B. in a prison that is not overcrowded there will not be any problems of order and discipline
C. it is undesirable for the inmate population to exceed unduly the intended capacity of a prison
D. segregation of prisoners is carried on mainly for the purpose of better prison administration

22. Most non-professional shoplifters are women of comfortable means who could buy the things they steal. Of the following, the MOST valid conclusion which can be drawn from the preceding statement is that 22.____

A. some well-to-do women are shoplifters
B. most professional shoplifters are men
C. few women practice shoplifting as a profession
D. most shoplifters suffer from a mental ailment rather than from a moral deficiency

23. Since accomplices and instigators are harder to detect and successfully prosecute than overt perpetrators, most women offenders therefore escape punishment. Of the following, the MOST valid conclusion which can be drawn from the preceding statement is that 23.____

A. judges deal more leniently with female than with male offenders
B. men who are accomplices or instigators of crimes are easier to detect and prosecute than women
C. successful prosecution of women offenders depends to a large extent on their successful detection
D. women are more often accomplices in, rather than actual perpetrators of, criminal acts

24. Through the juvenile court, the recognition of social responsibility in the delinquent acts of an individual has been established. 24.____
The MOST accurate of the following statements on the basis of the preceding statement is that

A. delinquent behavior is an evidence of an individual's social irresponsibility
B. some individuals are responsible for their delinquent acts
C. the juvenile court is evidence of society's willingness to assume some blame for the anti-social behavior of its younger members
D. the juvenile court takes into consideration the age, social background, and offense of the individual before deciding upon his punishment

25. The way to win more offenders to lasting good behavior is to provide treatment to each offender based on an understanding of the causes of his actions and of his emotional needs in the light of modern insight into human nature. Of the following, the MOST valid inference which can be drawn from the preceding statement is that 25.____

A. few offenders are reformed today because they are not led to an understanding of the causes of their criminal actions
B. individualized attention is required to achieve reform in criminals
C. penologists have a better understanding of the causes of criminal behavior because of recent developments in the study of human nature
D. unsolved emotional conflicts frequently result in criminal acts

---

KEY (CORRECT ANSWERS)

1. A	11. B
2. B	12. D
3. A	13. A
4. C	14. B
5. B	15. C
6. C	16. D
7. A	17. B
8. C	18. D
9. A	19. D
10. D	20. C

21. C
22. A
23. D
24. C
25. B

DOCUMENTS AND FORMS
PREPARING WRITTEN MATERIAL
EXAMINATION SECTION

TEST 1

DIRECTIONS: Each question or incomplete statement is followed by several suggested answers or completions. Select the one that BEST answers the question or completes the statement. *PRINT THE LETTER OF THE CORRECT ANSWER IN THE SPACE AT THE RIGHT.*

1. Suppose that one of the forms you fill out daily requires some information which you know is unnecessary. 1.____
Which is the BEST action to take?
   A. Refuse to supply the information you think is unnecessary.
   B. Continue to fill out the form as required, even though the information is unnecessary.
   C. Suggest to your supervisor that the form be revised to reflect useful information.
   D. Suggest that fewer copies of the form be required.

2. Of the following, the MOST likely reason for recommending that your department establish a standard form for recording certain information would be that this information 2.____
   A. will be produced at some disciplinary hearing
   B. concerns a secret or confidential record about an unusual incident at the garage
   C. contains a detailed explanation of a complex procedure
   D. must be taken from a large number of people on a regular basis

3. If the four steps listed below for processing records were given in logical sequence, the one that would be the THIRD step is 3.____
   A. coding the records, using a chart or classification system
   B. inspecting the records to make sure they have been released for filing
   C. preparing cross-reference sheets or cards
   D. skimming the records to determine filing captions

4. Which of the following BEST describes "office work simplification"? 4.____
   A. An attempt to increase the rate of production by speeding up the movements of employees
   B. Eliminating wasteful steps in order to increase efficiency
   C. Making jobs as easy as possible for employees so they will not be overworked
   D. Eliminating all difficult tasks from an office and leaving only simple ones

5. The use of the same method of recordkeeping and reporting by all sections is 5.____
   A. *desirable*, mainly because it saves time in section operations
   B. *undesirable*, mainly because it kills the initiative of the individual section foreman
   C. *desirable*, mainly because it will be easier for the superior to evaluate and compare section operations
   D. *undesirable*, mainly because operations vary from section to section and uniform recordkeeping and reporting is not appropriate

6. The GREATEST benefit the section officer will have from keeping complete and accurate records of section operations is that 6.____
   A. he will find it easier to run his section efficiently
   B. he will need less equipment
   C. he will need less manpower
   D. the section will run smoothly when he is out

7. You have prepared a report to your superior and are ready to send it forward. But on reading it, you think some parts are not clearly expressed and the superior may have difficulty getting your point. 7.____
   Of the following, it would be BEST for you to
   A. give the report to one of your men to read, and, if he has no trouble understanding it, send it through
   B. forward the report and call the superior the next day to ask if it was all right
   C. forward the report as is; higher echelons should be able to understand any report prepared by a section officer
   D. do the report over, re-writing the sections you are doubtful of

8. Of the following, a flow chart is BEST described as a chart which shows 8.____
   A. the places through which work moves in the course of the job process
   B. which employees perform specific functions leading to the completion of a job
   C. the schedules for production and how they eliminate waiting time between jobs
   D. how work units are affected by the actions of related work units

9. A superior decided to hold a problem-solving conference with his entire staff and distributed an announcement and agenda one week before the meeting. Of the following, the BEST reason for providing each participate with an agenda is that 9.____
   A. participants will feel that something will be accomplished
   B. participants may prepare for the conference
   C. controversy will be reduced
   D. the top man should state the expected conclusions

10. The one of the following activities which is generally the LEAST proper function of a centralized procedures section is 10.____
   A. issuing new and revised procedural instructions
   B. coordinating forms revision and procedural changes
   C. accepting or rejecting authorized procedural changes
   D. controlling standard numbering systems for procedural releases

11. Assume that it is the policy of an operating unit to act on all requests received within five working days. Several operations are involved in acting on these requests. Each operation is performed by a separate sub-unit. The staff of the unit is reasonable adequate to handle this workload. 11.____
If only one of the following can be done, the MOST effective procedure for maintaining adherence to the unit's five-day processing policy is to
   A. maintain a central "tickler" file in each sub-unit for the requests received daily in that sub-unit
   B. prepare a "tickler" card for each request and follow it up five days later to determine whether action has been taken
   C. rely on standards of production for each operation as an incentive to the employees of each sub-unit to meet the schedule
   D. schedule the operations on a timetable basis so that the request will be forwarded from one sub-unit to another within specified time limits

12. When one or two simple changes are needed in a memo to another unit or in a letter to a citizen, a unit head follows the practice of making such simple changes neatly in ink. 12.____
This practice is GENERALLY
   A. *poor*, chiefly because it reflects unfavorably on the originating unit's ability to make a decision
   B. *good*, chiefly because the department's public image is likely to be improved when people see it as trying to save money and speed up its processes
   C. *poor*, chiefly because a letter or document prepared in final form represents an investment of department time and effort and should go out only as a perfect finished product
   D. *good*, chiefly because the document may be important, and sending it back for retyping may delay it too long to achieve its purpose

13. Suppose that one of the office machines in your unit is badly in need of replacement. 13.____
Of the following, the MOST important reason for postponing immediate purchase of a new machine would be that
   A. a later model of the machine is expected on the market in a few months
   B. the new machine is more expensive than the old machine
   C. the operator of the present machine will have to be instructed by the manufacturer in the operation of the new machine
   D. the employee operating the old machine is not complaining

14. To avoid cutting off parts of letters when using an automatic letter opener, it is BEST to 14.____
   A. arrange all of the letters so that the addresses are right side up
   B. hold the envelopes up to the light to make sure their contents have not settled to the side that is to be opened
   C. strike the envelopes against a table or desktop several times so that the contents of all the envelopes settle to one side
   D. check the enclosures periodically to make sure that the machine has not been cutting into them

15. Of the following, the BEST reason for setting up a partitioned work area for the typists in our office is that 15.____
   A. an uninterrupted flow of work among the typists will be possible
   B. complaints about ventilation and lighting will be reduced
   C. the first-line supervisor will have more direct control over the typists
   D. the noise of the typewriters will be less disturbing to other workers

16. From the viewpoint of use of a typewriter to fill in a form, the MOST important design factor to consider is 16.____
   A. standard spacing
   B. box headings
   C. serial numbering
   D. vertical guide lines

17. Requests to repair office equipment which appears to be unsafe should be given priority MAINLY because, if repairs are delayed, 17.____
   A. there may be injuries to staff
   B. there may be further deterioration of the equipment
   C. work flow may be interrupted
   D. the cost of repair may increase

18. A clerk is asked to complete two assignments – transcribe a handwritten business letter and create a spreadsheet. Which two computer programs would the clerk use? 18.____
   A. Microsoft Word and Microsoft Excel
   B. Microsoft Word and Microsoft PowerPoint
   C. Google Docs and Google Chrome
   D. Adobe Reader and Microsoft PowerPoint

19. Generally, the actual floor space occupied by a standard letter-size office file cabinet, when closed, is MOST NEARLY 19.____
   A. ½ square foot
   B. 3 square feet
   C. 7 square feet
   D. 11 square feet

20. Suppose a clerk under your supervision accidentally opens a personal letter while handling office mail. 20.____
   Under such circumstances, you should tell the clerk to put the letter back into the envelope and
   A. take the letter to the person to whom it belongs and make sure he understands that the clerk did not read it
   B. try to seal the envelope so it won't appear to have been opened

C. write on the envelope "Sorry – opened by mistake," and put his initials on it
D. write on the envelope "Sorry – opened by mistake," but not put his initials on it

21. Standard forms frequently call for entries on them to be printed. The MAIN reason for this practice is that printing, as compared to writing, is GENERALLY 21.____
A. more compact
B. more legal
C. more legible
D. easier to do

22. After a stenographer types a letter which has been dictated, the finished letter should be carefully read for errors. If he dictator follows the procedure of carefully reading each transcribed letter, a stenographer, under your supervision, should, unless you instruct her otherwise 22.____
A. not take time to proofread transcribed letters
B. continue to carefully proofread transcribed letters
C. review transcribed letters for meaning rather than for errors in typing or transcription
D. review transcribed letters for errors in typing rather than for errors in transcription

23. In transcribing a letter, the secretary notes that the dictator said, "The series of conferences are planned to be relevant to today's problems." In such a case, the secretary should 23.____
A. type the sentence as it appears in the notes
B. check with the dictator to see whether he would prefer a different grammatical construction
C. change the noun so that it is correct
D. revise the sentence as much as necessary to make it read better

24. Of the following, the BEST procedure for your staff to follow in transcribing several letters that were dictated is to 24.____
A. transcribe first the letters that are most difficult so that they can return immediately to the dictator with any questions
B. read through the notes for each letter to be sure they have all the information needed before preparing the transcript
C. transcribe first those letters that are shortest and simplest in order to get them out of the way
D. read all the notes aloud to a co-worker to see whether they sound right

25. In typing long letters, which of the following is generally considered the LEAST desirable practice? 25.____
A. Numbering the second and succeeding pages of the letter
B. Typing a single line of a new paragraph as the last line of a page
C. Dividing a word at the end of a line of typing
D. Typing the name of the recipient of the letter on the second and succeeding pages

KEY (CORRECT ANSWERS)

1. C
2. D
3. D
4. B
5. C

6. A
7. D
8. A
9. B
10. C

11. D
12. B
13. A
14. C
15. D

16. A
17. A
18. A
19. B
20. C

21. C
22. B
23. B
24. B
25. B

TEST 2

DIRECTIONS: Each question or incomplete statement is followed by several suggested answers or completions. Select the one that BEST answers the question or completes the statement. *PRINT THE LETTER OF THE CORRECT ANSWER IN THE SPACE AT THE RIGHT.*

1. The use of a microfilm system for information storage and retrieval would make the MOST sense in an office where 1.____
   A. a great number of documents must be kept available for permanent reference
   B. documents are ordinarily kept on file for less than six months
   C. filing is a minor and unimportant part of the office work
   D. most of the records on file are working forms on which additional entries are frequently made

2. Of the following concepts, the one which CANNOT be represented suitably by a pie chart is 2.____
   A. percent shares
   B. shares in absolute units
   C. time trends
   D. successive totals over time, with their shares

3. A pictogram is ESSENTIALLY another version of a(n) _____ chart. 3.____
   A. plain bar
   B. component bar
   C. pie
   D. area

4. A time series for a certain cost is presented in a graph. It is drawn so that the vertical (cost) axis starts at a point well above zero. This is a legitimate method of presentation for some purposes, but it may have the effect of 4.____
   A. hiding fixed components of the cost
   B. exaggerating changes which, in actual amounts, may be insignificant
   C. minimizing variable components of the cost
   D. impairing correlation analysis

5. Certain budgetary data may be represented by bar, area, or volume charts. Which one of the following BEST expressed the most appropriate order of usefulness? 5.____
   A. Descends from bar to volume and area charts, the last two being about the same
   B. Descends from volume to area, to bar charts
   C. Depends on the nature of the data presented
   D. Descends from bar to area to volume charts

6. One weekend, you develop a painful infection in one hand. You know that your typing speed will be much slower than normal and the likelihood of your making mistakes will be increased. 6.____
Of the following, the BEST course of action for you to take in this situation is to
   A. report to work as scheduled and do your typing assignments as best you can without complaining
   B. report to work as scheduled and ask your co-workers to divide your typing assignments until your hand heals
   C. report to work as scheduled and ask your supervisor for non-typing assignments until your hand heals
   D. call in sick and remain on medical leave until your hand is completely healed so that you can perform your normal duties

7. When filling out a departmental form during an interview concerning a citizen complaint, an interviewer should know the purpose of each question that he asks the citizen. For such information to be supplied by your department is 7.____
   A. *advisable*, because the interviewer may lose interest in the job if he is not fully informed about the questions he has to ask
   B. *inadvisable*, because the interviewer may reveal the true purpose of the questions to the citizens
   C. *advisable*, because the interviewer might otherwise record superficial or inadequate answers if he does not fully understand the questions
   D. *inadvisable*, because the information obtained through the form may be of little importance to the interviewer

8. The one of the following which is the BEST reason for placing the date and time of receipt on incoming mail is that this procedure 8.____
   A. aids the filing of correspondence in alphabetical order
   B. fixes responsibility for promptness in answering correspondence
   C. indicates that the mail has been checked for the presence of a return address
   D. makes it easier to distribute the main in sequence

9. Which one of the following is the FIRST step that you should take when filing a document by subject? 9.____
   A. Arrange related documents by date with the latest date in front
   B. Check whether the document has been released for filing
   C. Cross-reference the document if necessary
   D. Determine the category under which the document will be filed

10. The one of the following which is NOT generally employed to keep track of frequently used material requiring future attention is a 10.____
   A. card tickler file
   B. dated follow-up folder
   C. periodic transferal of records
   D. signal folder

11. Which one of the following is NOT a useful filing practice? 11.____
   A. Filing active records in the most accessible parts of the file cabinet
   B. Filing a file drawer to capacity in order to save space
   C. Gluing small documents to standard-size paper before filing
   D. Using different colored labels for various filing categories

12. The one of the following cases in which you would NOT place a special notation in the left margin of a letter that you have typed is when 12.____
   A. one of the copies is intended for someone other than the addressee of the letter
   B. you enclose a flyer with the letter
   C. you sign your superior's name to the letter, at his or her request
   D. the letter refers to something being sent under separate cover

13. Suppose that you accidentally cut a letter or enclosure as you are opening an envelope with a paper knife. The one of the following that you should do FIRST is to 13.____
   A. determine whether the document is important
   B. clip or staple the pieces together and process as usual
   C. mend the cut document with transparent tape
   D. notify the sender that the communication was damaged and request another copy

14. It is generally advisable to leave at least six inches of working space in a file drawer. This procedure is MOST useful in 14.____
   A. decreasing the number of filing errors
   B. facilitating the sorting of documents and folders
   C. maintaining a regular program of removing inactive records
   D. preventing folders and papers from being torn

15. Of the following, the MOST important reason to sort large volumes of documents before filing is that sorting 15.____
   A. decreases the need for cross-referencing
   B. eliminates the need to keep the filing up-to-date
   C. prevents overcrowding of the file drawers
   D. saves time and energy in filing

16. When typing a preliminary draft of a report, the one of the following which you should generally NOT do is to 16.____
   A. erase typing errors and deletions rather than "X"ing them out
   B. leave plenty of room at the top, bottom, and sides of each page
   C. make only the number of copies that you are asked to make
   D. type double or triple space

17. When printing a 500-page office manual, the most efficient method is to use which of the following office machines? 17.____
   A. Inkjet printer
   B. Copy machine
   C. Word processor
   D. All-in-one scanner/fax/copier

18. When typing name or titles on a roll of folder labels, the one of the following which it is MOST important to do is to type the caption 18.____
   A. as it appears son the papers to be placed in the folder
   B. in capital letters
   C. in exact indexing or filing order
   D. so that it appears near the bottom of the folder tab when the label is attached

19. The MOST important reason for having color cartridges on hand for an office copier even though most prints are black and white is because 19.____
   A. color ink is used for all copies
   B. some copiers or printers will not print black and white if any of the color cartridges are empty
   C. black ink is cheaper when purchasing along with color cartridges
   D. lack of color ink can cause copier malfunctions

20. All of the following pertain to the formatting of word-processing documents EXCEPT 20.____
   A. headers and footers
   B. rows and columns
   C. indents and page breaks
   D. alignment and justified type

KEY (CORRECT ANSWERS)

1.	A	11.	B
2.	C	12.	C
3.	A	13.	C
4.	B	14.	D
5.	D	15.	D
6.	C	16.	A
7.	C	17.	B
8.	B	18.	C
9.	B	19.	B
10.	C	20.	B

PREPARING WRITTEN MATERIALS

EXAMINATION SECTION
TEST 1

DIRECTIONS: Each question or incomplete statement is followed by several suggested answers or completions. Select the one that BEST answers the question or completes the statement. *PRINT THE LETTER OF THE CORRECT ANSWER IN THE SPACE AT THE RIGHT.*

Questions 1-25.

DIRECTIONS: Questions 1 through 25 consist of sentences which may or may not be examples of good English usage. Consider grammar, punctuation, spelling, capitalization, awkwardness, etc. Examine each sentence, and then choose the correct statement about it from the four choices below it. If the English usage in the sentence given is better than it would be with any of the changes suggested in options B, C, and D, choose option A. Do not choose an option that will change the meaning of the sentence.

1. According to Judge Frank, the grocer's sons found guilty of assault and sentenced last Thursday. 1.____

   A. This is an example of acceptable writing.
   B. A comma should be placed after the word *sentenced.*
   C. The word *were* should be placed after *sons.*
   D. The apostrophe in grocer's should be placed after the *s.*

2. The department heads assistant said that the stenographers should type duplicate copies of all contracts, leases, and bills. 2.____

   A. This is an example of acceptable writing.
   B. A comma should be placed before the word *contracts.*
   C. An apostrophe should be placed before the *s* in *heads.*
   D. Quotation marks should be placed before *the stenographers* and after *bills.*

3. The lawyers questioned the men to determine who was the true property owner? 3.____

   A. This is an example of acceptable writing.
   B. The phrase *questioned the men* should be changed to *asked the men questions.*
   C. The word *was* should be changed to *were.*
   D. The question mark should be changed to a period.

4. The terms stated in the present contract are more specific than those stated in the previous contract. 4.____

   A. This is an example of acceptable writing.
   B. The word *are* should be changed to *is.*
   C. The word *than* should be changed to *then.*
   D. The word *specific* should be changed to *specified.*

5. Of the few lawyers considered, the one who argued more skillful was chosen for the job. 5.____

   A. This is an example of acceptable writing.
   B. The word *more* should be replaced by the word *most.*
   C. The word *skillful* should be replaced by the word *skillfully.*
   D. The word *chosen* should be replaced by the word *selected.*

6. Each of the states has a court of appeals; some states have circuit courts. 6.____

   A. This is an example of acceptable writing.
   B. The semi-colon should be changed to a comma.
   C. The word *has* should be changed to *have.*
   D. The word *some* should be capitalized.

7. The court trial has greatly effected the child's mental condition. 7.____

   A. This is an example of acceptable writing.
   B. The word *effected* should be changed to *affected.*
   C. The word *greatly* should be placed after *effected.*
   D. The apostrophe in *child's* should be placed after the *s.*

8. Last week, the petition signed by all the officers was sent to the Better Business Bureau. 8.____

   A. This is an example of acceptable writing.
   B. The phrase *last week* should be placed after *officers.*
   C. A comma should be placed after *petition.*
   D. The word *was* should be changed to *were.*

9. Mr. Farrell claims that he requested form A-12, and three booklets describing court procedures. 9.____

   A. This is an example of acceptable writing.
   B. The word *that* should be eliminated.
   C. A colon should be placed after *requested.*
   D. The comma after *A-12* should be eliminated.

10. We attended a staff conference on Wednesday the new safety and fire rules were discussed. 10.____

    A. This is an example of acceptable writing.
    B. The words *safety, fire,* and *rules* should begin with capital letters.
    C. There should be a comma after the word *Wednesday.*
    D. There should be a period after the word *Wednesday,* and the word *the* should begin with a capital letter.

11. Neither the dictionary or the telephone directory could be found in the office library. 11.____

    A. This is an example of acceptable writing.
    B. The word *or* should be changed to *nor.*
    C. The word *library* should be spelled *libery.*
    D. The word *neither* should be changed to *either.*

12. The report would have been typed correctly if the typist could read the draft. 12.____

    A. This is an example of acceptable writing.
    B. The word *would* should be removed.
    C. The word *have* should be inserted after the word *could.*
    D. The word *correctly* should be changed to *correct.*

13. The supervisor brought the reports and forms to an employees desk. 13.____

    A. This is an example of acceptable writing.
    B. The word *brought* should be changed to *took.*
    C. There should be a comma after the word *reports* and a comma after the word *forms.*
    D. The word *employees* should be spelled *employee's.*

14. It's important for all the office personnel to submit their vacation schedules on time. 14.____

    A. This is an example of acceptable writing.
    B. The word *It's* should be spelled *Its.*
    C. The word *their* should be spelled *they're.*
    D. The word *personnel* should be spelled *personal.*

15. The supervisor wants that all staff members report to the office at 9:00 A.M. 15.____

    A. This is an example of acceptable writing.
    B. The word *that* should be removed and the word *to* should be inserted after the word *members.*
    C. There should be a comma after the word *wants* and a comma after the word *office.*
    D. The word *wants* should be changed to *want*, and the word *shall* should be inserted after the word *members.*

16. Every morning the clerk opens the office mail and distributes it. 16.____

    A. This is an example of acceptable writing.
    B. The word *opens* should be changed to *open.*
    C. The word *mail* should be changed to *letters.*
    D. The word *it* should be changed to *them.*

17. The secretary typed more fast on a desktop computer than on a tablet. 17.____

    A. This is an example of acceptable writing.
    B. The words *more fast* should be changed to *faster.*
    C. There should be a comma after the words *desktop computer.*
    D. The word *than* should be changed to *then.*

18. The typist used an extention cord in order to connect her typewriter to the outlet nearest to her desk. 18.____

    A. This is an example of acceptable writing.
    B. A period should be placed after the word *cord,* and the word *in* should have a capital *I.*
    C. A comma should be placed after the word *typewriter.*
    D. The word *extention* should be spelled *extension.*

19. He would have went to the conference if he had received an invitation. 19.____

A. This is an example of acceptable writing.
B. The word *went* should be replaced by the word *gone.*
C. The word *had* should be replaced by *would have.*
D. The word *conference* should be spelled *conferance.*

20. In order to make the report neater, he spent many hours rewriting it. 20.____

A. This is an example of acceptable writing.
B. The word *more* should be inserted before the word *neater.*
C. There should be a colon after the word *neater.*
D. The word *spent* should be changed to *have spent.*

21. His supervisor told him that he should of read the memorandum more carefully. 21.____

A. This is an example of acceptable writing.
B. The word *memorandum* should be spelled *memorandom.*
C. The word *of* should be replaced by the word *have.*
D. The word *carefully* should be replaced by the word *careful.*

22. It was decided that two separate reports should be written. 22.____

A. This is an example of acceptable writing.
B. A comma should be inserted after the word *decided.*
C. The word *be* should be replaced by the word *been.*
D. A colon should be inserted after the word *that.*

23. She don't seem to understand that the work must be done as soon as possible. 23.____

A. This is an example of acceptable writing.
B. The word *doesn't* should replace the word *don't.*
C. The word *why* should replace the word *that.*
D. The word *as* before the word *soon* should be eliminated.

24. He excepted praise from his supervisor for a job well done. 24.____

A. This is an example of acceptable writing.
B. The word *excepted* should be spelled *accepted.*
C. The order of the words *well done* should be changed to *done well.*
D. There should be a comma after the word *supervisor.*

25. What appears to be intentional errors in grammar occur several times in the passage. 25.____

A. This is an example of acceptable writing.
B. The word *occur* should be spelled *occurr.*
C. The word *appears* should be changed to *appear.*
D. The phrase *several times* should be changed to *from time to time.*

KEY (CORRECT ANSWERS)

1. C
2. C
3. D
4. A
5. C

6. A
7. B
8. A
9. D
10. D

11. B
12. C
13. D
14. A
15. B

16. A
17. B
18. D
19. B
20. A

21. C
22. A
23. B
24. B
25. C

TEST 2

DIRECTIONS: Each question consists of a sentence which may or may not be an example of good formal English usage. Examine each sentence, considering grammar, punctuation, spelling, capitalization, and awkwardness. Then choose the CORRECT statement about it from the four options below it. If the English usage in the sentence given is better than any of the changes suggested in options B, C, or D, pick option A. Do not pick an option that will change the meaning of the sentence. *PRINT THE LETTER OF THE CORRECT ANSWER IN THE SPACE AT THE RIGHT.*

1. I don't know who could possibly of broken it. 1.____

   A. This is an example of acceptable writing.
   B. The word *who* should be replaced by the word *whom.*
   C. The word *of* should be replaced by the word *have.*
   D. The word *broken* should be replaced by the word *broke.*

2. Telephoning is easier than to write. 2.____

   A. This is an example of acceptable writing.
   B. The word *telephoning* should be spelled *telephoneing.*
   C. The word *than* should be replaced by the word *then.*
   D. The words *to write* should be replaced by the word *writing.*

3. The two operators who have been assigned to these consoles are on vacation. 3.____

   A. This is an example of acceptable writing.
   B. A comma should be placed after the word *operators.*
   C. The word *who* should be replaced by the word *whom*
   D. The word *are* should be replaced by the word *is.*

4. You were suppose to teach me how to operate a plugboard. 4.____

   A. This is an example of acceptable writing.
   B. The word *were* should be replaced by the word *was.*
   C. The word *suppose* should be replaced by the word *supposed.*
   D. The word *teach* should be replaced by the word *learn.*

5. If you had taken my advice; you would have spoken with him. 5.____

   A. This is an example of acceptable writing.
   B. The word *advice* should be spelled *advise.*
   C. The words *had taken* should be replaced by the word *take.*
   D. The semicolon should be changed to a comma.

6. The clerk could have completed the assignment on time if he knows where these materials were located. 6.____

   A. This is an example of acceptable writing.
   B. The word *knows* should be replaced by *had known.*
   C. The word *were* should be replaced by *had been.*
   D. The words *where these materials were located* should be replaced by *the location of these materials.*

7. All employees should be given safety training. Not just those who have accidents. 7.____

   A. This is an example of acceptable writing.
   B. The period after the word *training* should be changed to a colon.
   C. The period after the word *training* should be changed to a semicolon, and the first letter of the word *Not* should be changed to a small *n.*
   D. The period after the word *training* should be changed to a comma, and the first letter of the word *Not* should be changed to a small *n.*

8. This proposal is designed to promote employee awareness of the suggestion program, to encourage employee participation in the program, and to increase the number of suggestions submitted. 8.____

   A. This is an example of acceptable writing.
   B. The word *proposal* should be spelled *preposal.*
   C. The words *to increase the number of suggestions submitted* should be changed to *an increase in the number of suggestions is expected.*
   D. The word *promote* should be changed to *enhance,* and the word *increase* should be changed to *add to.*

9. The introduction of inovative managerial techniques should be preceded by careful analysis of the specific circumstances and conditions in each department. 9.____

   A. This is an example of acceptable writing.
   B. The word *techniques* should be spelled *techneques.*
   C. The word *inovative* should be spelled *innovative.*
   D. A comma should be placed after the word *circumstances* and after the word *conditions.*

10. This occurrence indicates that such criticism embarrasses him. 10.____

    A. This is an example of acceptable writing.
    B. The word *occurrence* should be spelled *occurence.*
    C. The word *criticism* should be spelled *criticism.*
    D. The word *embarrasses* should be spelled *embarasses.*

11. He can recommend a mechanic whose work is reliable. 11.____

    A. This is an example of acceptable writing.
    B. The word *reliable* should be spelled *relyable.*
    C. The word *whose* should be spelled *who's.*
    D. The word *mechanic* should be spelled *mecanic.*

12. She typed quickly; like someone who had not a moment to lose. 12.____

    A. This is an example of acceptable writing.
    B. The word *not* should be removed.
    C. The semicolon should be changed to a comma.
    D. The word *quickly* should be placed before instead of after the word *typed.*

13. She insisted that she had to much work to do. 13.____

    A. This is an example of acceptable writing.
    B. The word *insisted* should be spelled *insisted.*

C. The word *to* used in front of *much* should be spelled *too.*
D. The word *do* should be changed to *be done.*

14. The report, along with the accompanying documents, were submitted for review. 14.____

A. This is an example of acceptable writing.
B. The words *were submitted* should be changed to *was submitted.*
C. The word *accompanying* should be spelled *accompaning.*
D. The comma after the word *report* should be taken out.

15. If others must use your files, be certain that they understand how the system works, but insist that you do all the filing and refiling. 15.____

A. This is an example of acceptable writing.
B. There should be a period after the word *works,* and the word *but* should start a new sentence.
C. The words *filing* and *refiling* should be spelled *fileing* and *refileing.*
D. There should be a comma after the word *but.*

16. The appeal was not considered because of its late arrival. 16.____

A. This is an example of acceptable writing.
B. The word *its* should be changed to *it's.*
C. The word *its* should be changed to *the.*
D. The words *late arrival* should be changed to *arrival late.*

17. The letter must be read carefuly to determine under which subject it should be filed. 17.____

A. This is an example of acceptable writing.
B. The word *under* should be changed to *at.*
C. The word *determine* should be spelled *determin.*
D. The word *carefuly* should be spelled *carefully.*

18. He showed potential as an office manager, but he lacked skill in delegating work. 18.____

A. This is an example of acceptable writing.
B. The word *delegating* should be spelled *delagating.*
C. The word *potential* should be spelled *potencial.*
D. The words *he lacked* should be changed to *was lacking.*

19. His supervisor told him that it would be all right to receive personal mail at the office. 19.____

A. This is an example of acceptable writing.
B. The words *all right* should be changed to *alright.*
C. The word *personal* should be spelled *personel.*
D. The word *mail* should be changed to *letters.*

20. The report, along with the accompanying documents, were submitted for review. 20.____

A. This is an example of acceptable writing.
B. The words *were submitted* should be changed to *was submitted.*
C. The word *accompanying* should be spelled *accompaning.*
D. The comma after the word *report* should be taken out.

KEY (CORRECT ANSWERS)

1.	C	11.	A
2.	D	12.	C
3.	A	13.	C
4.	C	14.	B
5.	D	15.	A
6.	B	16.	A
7.	D	17.	D
8.	A	18.	A
9.	C	19.	A
10.	A	20.	B

PREPARING WRITTEN MATERIALS

EXAMINATION SECTION
TEST 1

DIRECTIONS: Each of the following questions consists of a sentence which may be classified appropriately under one of the following four categories:
A. Incorrect because of faulty grammar or sentence structure
B. Incorrect because of faulty punctuation
C. Incorrect because of faulty spelling or capitalization
D. Correct

Examine each sentence carefully. Then, in the space at the right, print the letter preceding the best of the four alternatives suggested above. All incorrect sentences contain but one type of error. Consider a sentence correct if it contains none of the types of errors mentioned, even though there may be other correct ways of expressing the same thought.

1. The fire apparently started in the storeroom, which is usually locked. 1.____
2. On approaching the victim two bruises were noticed by this officer. 2.____
3. The officer, who was there examined the report with great care. 3.____
4. Each employee in the office had a separate desk. 4.____
5. Each employee in the office had a separate desk. 5.____
6. The suggested procedure is similar to the one now in use. 6.____
7. No one was more pleased with the new procedure than the chauffeur. 7.____
8. He tried to pursuade her to change the procedure. 8.____
9. The total of the expenses charged to petty cash were high. 9.____
10. An understanding between him and I was finally reached. 10.____
11. It was at the supervisor's request that the clerk agreed to postpone his vacation. 11.____
12. We do not believe that it is necessary for both he and the clerk to attend the conference. 12.____
13. All employees, who display perseverance, will be given adequate recognition. 13.____
14. He regrets that some of us employees are dissatisfied with our new assignments. 14.____
15. "Do you think that the raise was merited," asked the supervisor? 15.____
16. The new manual of procedure is a valuable supplament to our rules and regulation. 16.____
17. The typist admitted that she had attempted to pursuade the other employees to assist her in her work. 17.____

18. The supervisor asked that all amendments to the regulations be handled by you and I. 18.____

19. They told both he and I that the prisoner had escaped. 19.____

20. Any superior officer, who, disregards the just complaints of his subordinates, is remiss in the performance of his duty. 20.____

21. Only those members of the national organization who resided in the Middle west attended the conference in Chicago. 21.____

22. We told him to give the investigation assignment to whoever was available. 22.____

23. Please do not disappoint and embarass us by not appearing in court. 23.____

24. Despite the efforts of the Supervising mechanic, the elevator could not be started. 24.____

25. The U.S. Weather Bureau, weather record for the accident date was checked. 25.____

KEY (CORRECT ANSWERS)

1. D
2. A
3. B
4. D
5. B

6. C
7. D
8. C
9. A
10. A

11. D
12. A
13. B
14. D
15. B

16. C
17. C
18. A
19. A
20. B

21. C
22. D
23. C
24. C
25. B

TEST 2

DIRECTIONS: Each question consists of a sentence. Some of the sentences contain errors in English grammar or usage, punctuation, spelling, or capitalization. A sentence does not contain an error simply because it could be written in a different manner. Choose answer

A. If the sentence contains an error in English grammar or usage
B. If the sentence contains an error in punctuation
C. If the sentence contains an error in spelling or capitalization
D. If the sentence does not contain any errors.

1. The severity of the sentence prescribed by contemporary statutes - including both the former and the revised New York Penal Laws - do not depend on what crime was intended by the offender. 1.____

2. It is generally recognized that two defects in the early law of attempt played a part in the birth of burglary: (1) immunity from prosecution for conduct short of the last act before completion of the crime, and (2) the relatively minor penalty imposed for an attempt (it being a common law misdemeanor) vis-a-vis the completed offense. 2.____

3. The first sentence of the statute is applicable to employees who enter their place of employment, invited guests, and all other persons who have an express or implied license or privilege to enter the premises. 3.____

4. Contemporary criminal codes in the United States generally divide burglary into various degrees, differentiating the categories according to place, time and other attendent circumstances. 4.____

5. The assignment was completed in record time but the payroll for it has not yet been preparid. 5.____

6. The operator, on the other hand, is willing to learn me how to use the mimeograph. 6.____

7. She is the prettiest of the three sisters. 7.____

8. She doesn't know; if the mail has arrived. 8.____

9. The doorknob of the office door is broke. 9.____

10. Although the department's supply of scratch pads and stationery have diminished considerably, the allotment for our division has not been reduced. 10.____

11. You have not told us whom you wish to designate as your secretary. 11.____

12. Upon reading the minutes of the last meeting, the new proposal was taken up for consideration. 12.____

13. Before beginning the discussion, we locked the door as a precautionery measure. 13.____

14. The supervisor remarked, "Only those clerks, who perform routine work, are permitted to take a rest period." 14.____

15. Not only will this duplicating machine make accurate copies, but it will also produce a quantity of work equal to fifteen transcribing typists. 15.____

16. "Mr. Jones," said the supervisor, "we regret our inability to grant you an extent ion of your leave of absence." 16.____

17. Although the employees find the work monotonous and fatigueing, they rarely complain. 17.____

18. We completed the tabulation of the receipts on time despite the fact that Miss Smith our fastest operator was absent for over a week. 18.____

19. The reaction of the employees who attended the meeting, as well as the reaction of those who did not attend, indicates clearly that the schedule is satisfactory to everyone concerned. 19.____

20. Of the two employees, the one in our office is the most efficient. 20.____

21. No one can apply or even understand, the new rules and regulations. 21.____

22. A large amount of supplies were stored in the empty office. 22.____

23. If an employee is occassionally asked to work overtime, he should do so willingly. 23.____

24. It is true that the new procedures are difficult to use but, we are certain that you will learn them quickly. 24.____

25. The office manager said that he did not know who would be given a large allotment under the new plan. 25.____

KEY (CORRECT ANSWERS)

1. A
2. D
3. D
4. C
5. C
6. A
7. D
8. B
9. A
10. A
11. D
12. A
13. C
14. B
15. A
16. C
17. C
18. B
19. D
20. A
21. B
22. A
23. C
24. B
25. D

TEST 3

DIRECTIONS: Each of the following sentences may be classified MOST appropriately under one of the following our categories:

A. faulty because of incorrect grammar;
B. faulty because of incorrect punctuation;
C. faulty because of incorrect capitalization;
D. correct

Examine each sentence carefully. Then, in the space at the right, print the capital letter preceding the option which is the BEST of the four suggested above. All incorrect sentences contain but one type of error. Consider a sentence correct if it contains none of the types of errors mentioned, even though there may be other correct ways of expressing the same thought.

1. The desk, as well as the chairs, were moved out of the office. 1.____

2. The clerk whose production was greatest for the month won a day's vacation as first prize. 2.____

3. Upon entering the room, the employees were found hard at work at their desks. 3.____

4. John Smith our new employee always arrives at work on time. 4.____

5. Punish whoever is guilty of stealing the money. 5.____

6. Intelligent and persistent effort lead to success no matter what the job may be. 6.____

7. The secretary asked, "can you call again at three o'clock?" 7.____

8. He told us, that if the report was not accepted at the next meeting, it would have to be rewritten. 8.____

9. He would not have sent the letter if he had known that it would cause so much excitement. 9.____

10. We all looked forward to him coming to visit us. 10.____

11. If you find that you are unable to complete the assignment please notify me as soon as possible. 11.____

12. Every girl in the office went home on time but me; there was still some work for me to finish. 12.____

13. He wanted to know who the letter was addressed to, Mr. Brown or Mr. Smith. 13.____

14. "Mr. Jones, he said, please answer this letter as soon as possible." 14.____

15. The new clerk had an unusual accent inasmuch as he was born and educated in the south. 15.____

16. Although he is younger than her, he earns a higher salary. 16.____

17. Neither of the two administrators are going to attend the conference being held in Washington, D.C. 17.____

18. Since Miss Smith and Miss Jones have more experience than us, they have been given more responsible duties. 18.____

19. Mr. Shaw the supervisor of the stock room maintains an inventory of stationery and office supplies. 19.____

20. Inasmuch as this matter affects both you and I, we should take joint action. 20.____

21. Who do you think will be able to perform this highly technical work? 21.____

22. Of the two employees, John is considered the most competent. 22.____

23. He is not coming home on tuesday; we expect him next week. 23.____

24. Stenographers, as well as typists must be able to type rapidly and accurately. 24.____

25. Having been placed in the safe we were sure that the money would not be stolen. 25.____

KEY (CORRECT ANSWERS)

1. A
2. D
3. A
4. B
5. D

6. A
7. C
8. A
9. D
10. A

11. B
12. D
13. A
14. B
15. C

16. A
17. A
18. A
19. B
20. A

21. D
22. A
23. C
24. B
25. A

TEST 4

DIRECTIONS: Each of the following sentences consist of four sentences lettered A, B, C, and D. One of the sentences in each group contains an error in grammar or punctuation. Indicate the INCORRECT sentence in each group. *PRINT THE LETTER OF THE CORRECT ANSWER IN THE SPACE AT THE RIGHT.*

1. A. Give the message to whoever is on duty. 1.____
   B. The teacher who's pupil won first prize presented the award.
   C. Between you and me, I don't expect the program to succeed.
   D. His running to catch the bus caused the accident.

2. A. The process, which was patented only last year is already obsolete. 2.____
   B. His interest in science (which continues to the present) led him to convert his basement into a laboratory.
   C. He described the book as "verbose, repetitious, and bombastic".
   D. Our new director will need to possess three qualities: vision, patience, and fortitude.

3. A. The length of ladder trucks varies considerably. 3.____
   B. The probationary fireman reported to the officer to whom he was assigned.
   C. The lecturer emphasized the need for we firemen to be punctual.
   D. Neither the officers nor the members of the company knew about the new procedure.

4. A. Ham and eggs is the specialty of the house. 4.____
   B. He is one of the students who are on probation.
   C. Do you think that either one of us have a chance to be nominated for president of the class?
   D. I assume that either he was to be in charge or you were.

5. A. Its a long road that has no turn. 5.____
   B. To run is more tiring than to walk.
   C. We have been assigned three new reports: namely, the statistical summary, the narrative summary, and the budgetary summary.
   D. Had the first payment been made in January, the second would be due in April.

6. A. Each employer has his own responsibilities. 6.____
   B. If a person speaks correctly, they make a good impression.
   C. Every one of the operators has had her vacation.
   D. Has anybody filed his report?

7. A. The manager, with all his salesmen, was obliged to go. 7.____
   B. Who besides them is to sign the agreement?
   C. One report without the others is incomplete.
   D. Several clerks, as well as the proprietor, was injured.

8. A. A suspension of these activities is expected. 8.____
   B. The machine is economical because first cost and upkeep are low.
   C. A knowledge of stenography and filing are required for this position.
   D. The condition in which the goods were received shows that the packing was not done properly.

9. A. There seems to be a great many reasons for disagreement. 9.____
   B. It does not seem possible that they could have failed.
   C. Have there always been too few applicants for these positions?
   D. There is no excuse for these errors.

10. A. We shall be pleased to answer your question. 10.____
    B. Shall we plan the meeting for Saturday?
    C. I will call you promptly at seven.
    D. Can I borrow your book after you have read it?

11. A. You are as capable as I. 11.____
    B. Everyone is willing to sign but him and me.
    C. As for he and his assistant, I cannot praise them too highly.
    D. Between you and me, I think he will be dismissed.

12. A. Our competitors bid above us last week. 12.____
    B. The survey which was began last year has not yet been completed.
    C. The operators had shown that they understood their instructions.
    D. We have never ridden over worse roads.

13. A. Who did they say was responsible? 13.____
    B. Whom did you suspect?
    C. Who do you suppose it was?
    D. Whom do you mean?

14. A. Of the two propositions, this is the worse. 14.____
    B. Which report do you consider the best -- the one in January or the one in July?
    C. I believe this is the most practicable of the many plans submitted.
    D. He is the youngest employee in the organization.

15. A. The firm had but three orders last week. 15.____
    B. That doesn't really seem possible.
    C. After twenty years scarcely none of the old business remains.
    D. Has he done nothing about it?

KEY (CORRECT ANSWERS)

1. B
2. A
3. C
4. C
5. A
6. B
7. D
8. C
9. A
10. D
11. C
12. B
13. A
14. B
15. C

PREPARING WRITTEN MATERIAL

PARAGRAPH REARRANGEMENT COMMENTARY

The sentences which follow are in scrambled order. You are to rearrange them in proper order and indicate the letter choice containing the correct answer at the space at the right.

Each group of sentences in this section is actually a paragraph presented in scrambled order. Each sentence in the group has a place in that paragraph; no sentence is to be left out. You are to read each group of sentences and decide upon the best order in which to put the sentences so as to form as well-organized paragraph.

The questions in this section measure the ability to solve a problem when all the facts relevant to its solution are not given.

More specifically, certain positions of responsibility and authority require the employee to discover connections between events sometimes, apparently, unrelated. In order to do this, the employee will find it necessary to correctly infer that unspecified events have probably occurred or are likely to occur. This ability becomes especially important when action must be taken on incomplete information.

Accordingly, these questions require competitors to choose among several suggested alternatives, each of which presents a different sequential arrangement of the events. Competitors must choose the MOST logical of the suggested sequences.

In order to do so, they may be required to draw on general knowledge to infer missing concepts or events that are essential to sequencing the given events. Competitors should be careful to infer only what is essential to the sequence. The plausibility of the wrong alternatives will always require the inclusion of unlikely events or of additional chains of events which are NOT essential to sequencing the given events.

It's very important to remember that you are looking for the best of the four possible choices, and that the best choice of all may not even be one of the answers you're given to choose from.

There is no one right way to solve these problems. Many people have found it helpful to first write out the order of the sentences, as they would have arranged them, on their scrap paper before looking at the possible answers. If their optimum answer is there, this can save them some time. If it isn't, this method can still give insight into solving the problem. Others find it most helpful to just go through each of the possible choices, contrasting each as they go along. You should use whatever method feels comfortable, and works, for you.

While most of these types of questions are not that difficult, we've added a higher percentage of the difficult type, just to give you more practice. Usually there are only one or two questions on this section that contain such subtle distinctions that you're unable to answer confidently, and you then may find yourself stuck deciding between two possible choices, neither of which you're sure about.

EXAMINATION SECTION
TEST 1

DIRECTIONS: The sentences that follow are in scrambled order. You are to rearrange them in proper order and indicate the letter choice containing the correct answer. *PRINT THE LETTER OF THE CORRECT ANSWER IN THE SPACE AT THE RIGHT.*

1. Below are four statements labeled W., X., Y., and Z. 1.____
   W. He was a strict and fanatic drillmaster.
   X. The word is always used in a derogatory sense and generally shows resentment and anger on the part of the user.
   Y. It is from the name of this Frenchman that we derive our English word, martinet.
   Z. Jean Martinet was the Inspector-General of Infantry during the reign of King Louis XIV.

   The *PROPER* order in which these sentences should be placed in a paragraph is:

   A. X, Z, W, Y B. X, Z, Y, W C. Z, W, Y, X D. Z, Y, W, X

2. In the following paragraph, the sentences which are numbered, have been jumbled. 2.____
   1. Since then it has undergone changes.
   2. It was incorporated in 1955 under the laws of the State of New York.
   3. Its primary purpose, a cleaner city, has, however, remained the same.
   4. The Citizens Committee works in cooperation with the Mayor's Inter-departmental Committee for a Clean City.

   The order in which these sentences should be arranged to form a well-organized paragraph is:

   A. 2, 4, 1, 3 B. 3, 4, 1, 2 C. 4, 2, 1, 3 D. 4, 3, 2, 1

Questions 3-5.

DIRECTIONS: The sentences listed below are part of a meaningful paragraph but they are not given in their proper order. You are to decide what would be the *best order* in which to put the sentences so as to form a well-organized paragraph. Each sentence has a place in the paragraph; there are no extra sentences. You are then to answer questions 3 to 5 inclusive on the basis of your rearrangements of these scrambled sentences into a properly organized paragraph.

In 1887 some insurance companies organized an Inspection Department to advise their clients on all phases of fire prevention and protection. Probably this has been due to the smaller annual fire losses in Great Britain than in the United States. It tests various fire prevention devices and appliances and determines manufacturing hazards and their safeguards. Fire research began earlier in the United States and is more advanced than in Great Britain. Later they established a laboratory specializing in electrical, mechanical, hydraulic, and chemical fields.

3. When the five sentences are arranged in proper order, the paragraph starts with the sentence which begins 3.____

   A. "In 1887..." B. "Probably this ..." C. "It tests ..."
   D. "Fire research ..." E. "Later they ..."

4. In the last sentence listed above, "they" refers to 4.____

   A. insurance companies
   B. the United States and Great Britain
   C. the Inspection Department
   D. clients
   E. technicians

5. When the above paragraph is properly arranged, it ends with the words 5.____

   A. "... and protection." B. "... the United States."
   C. "... their safeguards." D. "... in Great Britain."
   E. "... chemical fields."

KEY (CORRECT ANSWERS)

1. C
2. C
3. D
4. A
5. C

TEST 2

DIRECTIONS: In each of the questions numbered 1 through 5, several sentences are given. For each question, choose as your answer the group of numbers that represents the *most logical* order of these sentences if they were arranged in paragraph form. *PRINT THE LETTER OF THE CORRECT ANSWER IN THE SPACE AT THE RIGHT.*

1.
1. It is established when one shows that the landlord has prevented the tenant's enjoyment of his interest in the property leased. 1.____
2. Constructive eviction is the result of a breach of the covenant of quiet enjoyment implied in all leases.
3. In some parts of the United States, it is not complete until the tenant vacates within a reasonable time.
4. Generally, the acts must be of such serious and permanent character as to deny the tenant the enjoyment of his possessing rights.
5. In this event, upon abandonment of the premises, the tenant's liability for that ceases.

The CORRECT answer is:

A. 2, 1, 4, 3, 5 B. 5, 2, 3, 1, 4 C. 4, 3, 1, 2, 5
D. 1, 3, 5, 4, 2

2.
1. The powerlessness before private and public authorities that is the typical experience of the slum tenant is reminiscent of the situation of blue-collar workers all through the nineteenth century. 2.____
2. Similarly, in recent years, this chapter of history has been reopened by anti-poverty groups which have attempted to organize slum tenants to enable them to bargain collectively with their landlords about the conditions of their tenancies.
3. It is familiar history that many of the workers remedied their condition by joining together and presenting their demands collectively.
4. Like the workers, tenants are forced by the conditions of modern life into substantial dependence on these who possess great political arid economic power.
5. What's more, the very fact of dependence coupled with an absence of education and self-confidence makes them hesitant and unable to stand up for what they need from those in power.

The CORRECT answer is:

A. 5, 4, 1, 2, 3 B. 2, 3, 1, 5, 4 C. 3, 1, 5, 4, 2
D. 1, 4, 5, 3, 2

3.
1. A railroad, for example, when not acting as a common carrier may contract away responsibility for its own negligence. 3.____
2. As to a landlord, however, no decision has been found relating to the legal effect of a clause shifting the statutory duty of repair to the tenant.
3. The courts have not passed on the validity of clauses relieving the landlord of this duty and liability.
4. They have, however, upheld the validity of exculpatory clauses in other types of contracts.
5. Housing regulations impose a duty upon the landlord to maintain leased premises in safe condition.

6. As another example, a bailee may limit his liability except for gross negligence, willful acts, or fraud.

The CORRECT answer is:

A. 2, 1, 6, 4, 3, 5 B. 1, 3, 4, 5, 6, 2 C. 3, 5, 1, 4, 2, 6
D. 5, 3, 4, 1, 6, 2

4. 1. Since there are only samples in the building, retail or consumer sales are generally eschewed by mart occupants, and in some instances, rigid controls are maintained to limit entrance to the mart only to those persons engaged in retailing. 4.____
2. Since World War I, in many larger cities, there has developed a new type of property, called the mart building.
3. It can, therefore, be used by wholesalers and jobbers for the display of sample merchandise.
4. This type of building is most frequently a multi-storied, finished interior property which is a cross between a retail arcade and a loft building.
5. This limitation enables the mart occupants to ship the orders from another location after the retailer or dealer makes his selection from the samples.

The CORRECT answer is:

A. 2, 4, 3, 1, 5 B. 4, 3, 5, 1, 2 C. 1, 3, 2, 4, 5
D. 1, 4, 2, 3, 5

5. 1. In general, staff-line friction reduces the distinctive contribution of staff personnel. 5.____
2. The conflicts, however, introduce an uncontrolled element into the managerial system.
3. On the other hand, the natural resistance of the line to staff innovations probably usefully restrains over-eager efforts to apply untested procedures on a large scale.
4. Under such conditions, it is difficult to know when valuable ideas are being sacrificed.
5. The relatively weak position of staff, requiring accommodation to the line, tends to restrict their ability to engage in free, experimental innovation.

The CORRECT answer is:

A. 4, 2, 3, 1, 3 B. 1, 5, 3, 2, 4 C. 5, 3, 1, 2, 4
D. 2, 1, 4, 5, 3

KEY (CORRECT ANSWERS)

1. A
2. D
3. D
4. A
5. B

TEST 3

DIRECTIONS: Questions 1 through 4 consist of six sentences which can be arranged in a logical sequence. For each question, select the choice which places the numbered sentences in the *most logical* sequence. *PRINT THE LETTER OF THE CORRECT ANSWER IN THE SPACE AT THE RIGHT.*

1.
1. The burden of proof as to each issue is determined before trial and remains upon the same party throughout the trial. 1.____
2. The jury is at liberty to believe one witness' testimony as against a number of contradictory witnesses.
3. In a civil case, the party bearing the burden of proof is required to prove his contention by a fair preponderance of the evidence.
4. However, it must be noted that a fair preponderance of evidence does not necessarily mean a greater number of witnesses.
5. The burden of proof is the burden which rests upon one of the parties to an action to persuade the trier of the facts, generally the jury, that a proposition he asserts is true.
6. If the evidence is equally balanced, or if it leaves the jury in such doubt as to be unable to decide the controversy either way, judgment must be given against the party upon whom the burden of proof rests.

The CORRECT answer is:

A. 3, 2, 5, 4, 1, 6 B. 1, 2, 6, 5, 3, 4 C. 3, 4, 5, 1, 2, 6
D. 5, 1, 3, 6, 4, 2

2.
1. If a parent is without assets and is unemployed, he cannot be convicted of the crime of non-support of a child. 2.____
2. The term "sufficient ability" has been held to mean sufficient financial ability.
3. It does not matter if his unemployment is by choice or unavoidable circumstances.
4. If he fails to take any steps at all, he may be liable to prosecution for endangering the welfare of a child.
5. Under the penal law, a parent is responsible for the support of his minor child only if the parent is "of sufficient ability."
6. An indigent parent may meet his obligation by borrowing money or by seeking aid under the provisions of the Social Welfare Law.

The CORRECT answer is:

A. 6, 1, 5, 3, 2, 4 B. 1, 3, 5, 2, 4, 6 C. 5, 2, 1, 3, 6, 4
D. 1, 6, 4, 5, 2, 3

3. 1. Consider, for example, the case of a rabble rouser who urges a group of twenty people to go out and break the windows of a nearby factory. 3.____
   2. Therefore, the law fills the indicated gap with the crime of inciting to riot.
   3. A person is considered guilty of inciting to riot when he urges ten or more persons to engage in tumultuous and violent conduct of a kind likely to create public alarm.
   4. However, if he has not obtained the cooperation of at least four people, he cannot be charged with unlawful assembly.
   5. The charge of inciting to riot was added to the law to cover types of conduct which cannot be classified as either the crime of "riot" or the crime of "unlawful assembly."
   6. If he acquires the acquiescence of at least four of them, he is guilty of unlawful assembly even if the project does not materialize.

   The CORRECT answer is:

   A. 3, 5, 1, 6, 4, 2
   B. 5, 1, 4, 6, 2, 3
   C. 3, 4, 1, 5, 2, 6
   D. 5, 1, 4, 6, 3, 2

4. 1. If, however, the rebuttal evidence presents an issue of credibility, it is for the jury to determine whether the presumption has, in fact, been destroyed. 4.____
   2. Once sufficient evidence to the contrary is introduced, the presumption disappears from the trial.
   3. The effect of a presumption is to place the burden upon the adversary to come forward with evidence to rebut the presumption.
   4. When a presumption is overcome and ceases to exist in the case, the fact or facts which gave rise to the presumption still remain.
   5. Whether a presumption has been overcome is ordinarily a question for the court.
   6. Such information may furnish a basis for a logical inference.

   The CORRECT answer is:

   A. 4, 6, 2, 5, 1, 3
   B. 3, 2, 5, 1, 4, 6
   C. 5, 3, 6, 4, 2, 1
   D. 5, 4, 1, 2, 6, 3

KEY (CORRECT ANSWERS)

1. D
2. C
3. A
4. B

PHILOSOPHY, PRINCIPLES, PRACTICES AND TECHNICS OF SUPERVISION, ADMINISTRATION, MANAGEMENT AND ORGANIZATION

TABLE OF CONTENTS

TABLE OF CONTENTS (CONTINUED)

PHILOSOPHY, PRINCIPLES, PRACTICES, AND TECHNICS OF SUPERVISION, ADMINISTRATION, MANAGEMENT AND ORGANIZATION

I. MEANING OF SUPERVISION

The extension of the democratic philosophy has been accompanied by an extension in the scope of supervision. Modern leaders and supervisors no longer think of supervision in the narrow sense of being confined chiefly to visiting employees, supplying materials, or rating the staff. They regard supervision as being intimately related to all the concerned agencies of society, they speak of the supervisor's function in terms of "growth", rather than the "improvement," of employees.

This modern concept of supervision may be defined as follows:

Supervision is leadership and the development of leadership within groups which are cooperatively engaged in inspection, research, training, guidance and evaluation.

II. THE OLD AND THE NEW SUPERVISION

TRADITIONAL

1. Inspection
2. Focused on the employee
3. Visitation
4. Random and haphazard
5. Imposed and authoritarian
6. One person usually

MODERN

1. Study and analysis
2. Focused on aims, materials, methods, supervisors, employees, environment
3. Demonstrations, intervisitation, workshops, directed reading, bulletins, etc.
4. Definitely organized and planned (scientific)
5. Cooperative and democratic
6. Many persons involved (creative)

III THE EIGHT (8) BASIC PRINCIPLES OF THE NEW SUPERVISION

1. *PRINCIPLE OF RESPONSIBILITY*

   Authority to act and responsibility for acting must be joined.

   a. If you give responsibility, give authority.
   b. Define employee duties clearly.
   c. Protect employees from criticism by others.
   d. Recognize the rights as well as obligations of employees.
   e. Achieve the aims of a democratic society insofar as it is possible within the area of your work.
   f. Establish a situation favorable to training and learning.
   g. Accept ultimate responsibility for everything done in your section, unit, office, division, department.
   h. Good administration and good supervision are inseparable.

2. *PRINCIPLE OF AUTHORITY*

The success of the supervisor is measured by the extent to which the power of authority is not used.

a. Exercise simplicity and informality in supervision.
b. Use the simplest machinery of supervision.
c. If it is good for the organization as a whole, it is probably justified.
d. Seldom be arbitrary or authoritative.
e. Do not base your work on the power of position or of personality.
f. Permit and encourage the free expression of opinions.

3. *PRINCIPLE OF SELF-GROWTH*

The success of the supervisor is measured by the extent to which, and the speed with which, he is no longer needed.

a. Base criticism on principles, not on specifics.
b. Point out higher activities to employees.
c. Train for self-thinking by employees, to meet new situations.
d. Stimulate initiative, self-reliance and individual responsibility.
e. Concentrate on stimulating the growth of employees rather than on removing defects.

4. *PRINCIPLE OF INDIVIDUAL WORTH*

Respect for the individual is a paramount consideration in supervision.

a. Be human and sympathetic in dealing with employees.
b. Don't nag about things to be done.
c. Recognize the individual differences among employees and seek opportunities to permit best expression of each personality.

5. *PRINCIPLE OF CREATIVE LEADERSHIP*

The best supervision is that which is not apparent to the employee.

a. Stimulate, don't drive employees to creative action.
b. Emphasize doing good things.
c. Encourage employees to do what they do best.
d. Do not be too greatly concerned with details of subject or method.
e. Do not be concerned exclusively with immediate problems and activities.
f. Reveal higher activities and make them both desired and maximally possible.
g. Determine procedures in the light of each situation but see that these are derived from a sound basic philosophy.
h. Aid, inspire and lead so as to liberate the creative spirit latent in all good employees.

6. *PRINCIPLE OF SUCCESS AND FAILURE*

There are no unsuccessful employees, only unsuccessful supervisors who have failed to give proper leadership.

a. Adapt suggestions to the capacities, attitudes, and prejudices of employees.
b. Be gradual, be progressive, be persistent.
c. Help the employee find the general principle; have the employee apply his own problem to the general principle.
d. Give adequate appreciation for good work and honest effort.
e. Anticipate employee difficulties and help to prevent them.
f. Encourage employees to do the desirable things they will do anyway.
g. Judge your supervision by the results it secures.

7. *PRINCIPLE OF SCIENCE*

Successful supervision is scientific, objective, and experimental. It is based on facts, not on prejudices.

a. Be cumulative in results.
b. Never divorce your suggestions from the goals of training.
c. Don't be impatient of results.
d. Keep all matters on a professional, not a personal level.
e. Do not be concerned exclusively with immediate problems and activities.
f. Use objective means of determining achievement and rating where possible.

8. *PRINCIPLE OF COOPERATION*

Supervision is a cooperative enterprise between supervisor and employee.

a. Begin with conditions as they are.
b. Ask opinions of all involved when formulating policies.
c. Organization is as good as its weakest link.
d. Let employees help to determine policies and department programs.
e. Be approachable and accessible - physically and mentally.
f. Develop pleasant social relationships.

IV. WHAT IS ADMINISTRATION?

Administration is concerned with providing the environment, the material facilities, and the operational procedures that will promote the maximum growth and development of supervisors and employees. (Organization is an aspect, and a concomitant, of administration.)

There is no sharp line of demarcation between supervision and administration; these functions are intimately interrelated and, often, overlapping. They are complementary activities.

1. *PRACTICES COMMONLY CLASSED AS "SUPERVISORY"*

a. Conducting employees conferences
b. Visiting sections, units, offices, divisions, departments
c. Arranging for demonstrations
d. Examining plans
e. Suggesting professional reading
f. Interpreting bulletins
g. Recommending in-service training courses
h. Encouraging experimentation
i. Appraising employee morale
j. Providing for intervisitation

2. *PRACTICES COMMONLY CLASSIFIED AS "ADMINISTRATIVE"*

a. Management of the office
b. Arrangement of schedules for extra duties
c. Assignment of rooms or areas
d. Distribution of supplies
e. Keeping records and reports
f. Care of audio-visual materials
g. Keeping inventory records
h. Checking record cards and books
i. Programming special activities
j. Checking on the attendance and punctuality of employees

3. *PRACTICES COMMONLY CLASSIFIED AS BOTH "SUPERVISORY" AND "ADMINISTRATIVE"*
    a. Program construction
    b. Testing or evaluating outcomes
    c. Personnel accounting
    d. Ordering instructional materials

V. RESPONSIBILITIES OF THE SUPERVISOR

A person employed in a supervisory capacity must constantly be able to improve his own efficiency and ability. He represents the employer to the employees and only continuous self-examination can make him a capable supervisor.

Leadership and training are the supervisor's responsibility. An efficient working unit is one in which the employees work with the supervisor. It is his job to bring out the best in his employees. He must always be relaxed, courteous and calm in his association with his employees. Their feelings are important, and a harsh attitude does not develop the most efficient employees.

VI. COMPETENCIES OF THE SUPERVISOR

1. Complete knowledge of the duties and responsibilities of his position.
2. To be able to organize a job, plan ahead and carry through.
3. To have self-confidence and initiative.
4. To be able to handle the unexpected situation and make quick decisions.
5. To be able to properly train subordinates in the positions they are best suited for.
6. To be able to keep good human relations among his subordinates.
7. To be able to keep good human relations between his subordinates and himself and to earn their respect and trust.

VII. THE PROFESSIONAL SUPERVISOR-EMPLOYEE RELATIONSHIP

There are two kinds of efficiency: one kind is only apparent and is produced in organizations through the exercise of mere discipline; this is but a simulation of the second, or true, efficiency which springs from spontaneous cooperation. If you are a manager, no matter how great or small your responsibility, it is your job, in the final analysis, to create and develop this involuntary cooperation among the people whom you supervise. For, no matter how powerful a combination of money, machines, and materials a company may have, this is a dead and sterile thing without a team of willing, thinking and articulate people to guide it.

The following 21 points are presented as indicative of the exemplary basic relationship that should exist between supervisor and employee:

1. Each person wants to be liked and respected by his fellow employee and wants to be treated with consideration and respect by his superior.
2. The most competent employee will make an error. However, in a unit where good relations exist between the supervisor and his employees, tenseness and fear do not exist. Thus, errors are not hidden or covered up and the efficiency of a unit is not impaired.
3. Subordinates resent rules, regulations, or orders that are unreasonable or unexplained.
4. Subordinates are quick to resent unfairness, harshness, injustices and favoritism.
5. An employee will accept responsibility if he knows that he will be complimented for a job well done, and not too harshly chastised for failure; that his supervisor will check the cause of the failure, and, if it was the supervisor's fault, he will assume the blame therefore. If it was the employee's fault, his supervisor will explain the correct method or means of handling the responsibility.

6. An employee wants to receive credit for a suggestion he has made, that is used. If a suggestion cannot be used, the employee is entitled to an explanation. The supervisor should not say "no" and close the subject.
7. Fear and worry slow up a worker's ability. Poor working environment can impair his physical and mental health. A good supervisor avoids forceful methods, threats and arguments to get a job done.
8. A forceful supervisor is able to train his employees individually and as a team, and is able to motivate them in the proper channels.
9. A mature supervisor is able to properly evaluate his subordinates and to keep them happy and satisfied.
10. A sensitive supervisor will never patronize his subordinates.
11. A worthy supervisor will respect his employees' confidences.
12. Definite and clear-cut responsibilities should be assigned to each executive.
13. Responsibility should always be coupled with corresponding authority.
14. No change should be made in the scope or responsibilities of a position without a definite understanding to that effect on the part of all persons concerned.
15. No executive or employee, occupying a single position in the organization, should be subject to definite orders from more than one source.
16. Orders should never be given to subordinates over the head of a responsible executive. Rather than do this, the officer in question should be supplanted.
17. Criticisms of subordinates should, whoever possible, be made privately, and in no case should a subordinate be criticized in the presence of executives or employees of equal or lower rank.
18. No dispute or difference between executives or employees as to authority or responsibilities should be considered too trivial for prompt and careful adjudication.
19. Promotions, wage changes, and disciplinary action should always be approved by the executive immediately superior to the one directly responsible.
20. No executive or employee should ever be required, or expected, to be at the same time an assistant to, and critic of, another.
21. Any executive whose work is subject to regular inspection should, whever practicable, be given the assistance and facilities necessary to enable him to maintain an independent check of the quality of his work.

VIII. MINI-TEXT IN SUPERVISION, ADMINISTRATION, MANAGEMENT, AND ORGANIZATION

A. BRIEF HIGHLIGHTS

Listed concisely and sequentially are major headings and important data in the field for quick recall and review.

1. *LEVELS OF MANAGEMENT*

Any organization of some size has several levels of management. In terms of a ladder the levels are:

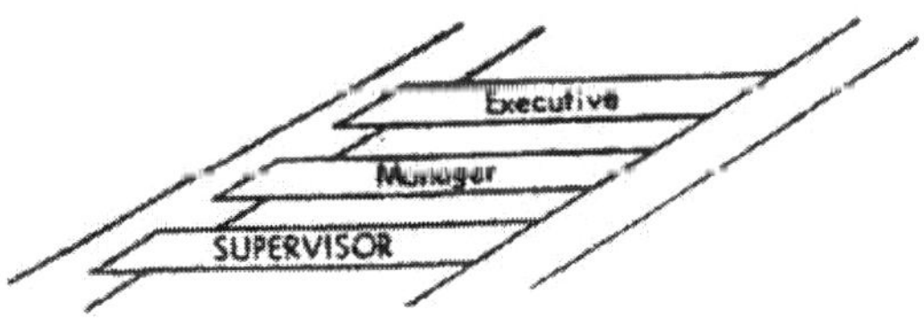

The first level is very important because it is the beginning point of management leadership.

2. *WHAT THE SUPERVISOR MUST LEARN*

A supervisor must learn to:

(1) Deal with people and their differences
(2) Get the job done through people
(3) Recognize the problems when they exist
(4) Overcome obstacles to good performance
(5) Evaluate the performance of people
(6) Check his own performance in terms of accomplishment

3. *A DEFINITION OF SUPERVISOR*

The term supervisor means any individual having authority, in the interests of the employer, to hire, transfer, suspend, lay-off, recall, promote, discharge, assign, reward, or discipline other employees or responsibility to direct them, or to adjust their grievances, or effectively to recommend such action, if, in connection with the foregoing, exercise of such authority is not of a merely routine or clerical nature but requires the use of independent judgment.

4. *ELEMENTS OF THE TEAM CONCEPT*

What is involved in teamwork? The component parts are:

(1) Members	(3) Goals	(5) Cooperation
(2) A leader	(4) Plans	(6) Spirit

5. *PRINCIPLES OF ORGANIZATION*

(1) A team member must know what his job is.
(2) Be sure that the nature and scope of a job are understood.
(3) Authority and responsibility should be carefully spelled out.
(4) A supervisor should be permitted to make the maximum number of decisions affecting his employees.
(5) Employees should report to only one supervisor.
(6) A supervisor should direct only as many employees as he can handle effectively.
(7) An organization plan should be flexible.
(8) Inspection and performance of work should be separate.
(9) Organizational problems should receive immediate attention.
(10) Assign work in line with ability and experience.

6. *THE FOUR IMPORTANT PARTS OF EVERY JOB*

(1) Inherent in every job is the *accountability* for results.
(2) A second set of factors in every job is *responsibilities.*
(3) Along with duties and responsibilities one must have the *authority* to act within certain limits without obtaining permission to proceed.
(4) No job exists in a vacuum. The supervisor is surrounded by key *relationships.*

7. *PRINCIPLES OF DELEGATION*

Where work is delegated for the first time, the supervisor should think in terms of these questions:

(1) Who is best qualified to do this?
(2) Can an employee improve his abilities by doing this?
(3) How long should an employee spend on this?
(4) Are there any special problems for which he will need guidance?
(5) How broad a delegation can I make?

8. *PRINCIPLES OF EFFECTIVE COMMUNICATIONS*
   (1) Determine the media
   (2) To whom directed?
   (3) Identification and source authority
   (4) Is communication understood?

9. *PRINCIPLES OF WORK IMPROVEMENT*
   (1) Most people usually do only the work which is assigned to them
   (2) Workers are likely to fit assigned work into the time available to perform it
   (3) A good workload usually stimulates output
   (4) People usually do their best work when they know that results will be reviewed or inspected
   (5) Employees usually feel that someone else is responsible for conditions of work, workplace layout, job methods, type of tools/equipment, and other such factors
   (6) Employees are usually defensive about their job security
   (7) Employees have natural resistance to change
   (8) Employees can support or destroy a supervisor
   (9) A supervisor usually earns the respect of his people through his personal example of diligence and efficiency

10. *AREAS OF JOB IMPROVEMENT*
    The areas of job improvement are quite numerous, but the most common ones which a supervisor can identify and utilize are:

(1) Departmental layout	(5) Work methods
(2) Flow of work	(6) Materials handling
(3) Workplace layout	(7) Utilization
(4) Utilization of manpower	(8) Motion economy

11. *SEVEN KEY POINTS IN MAKING IMPROVEMENTS*
    (1) Select the job to be improved
    (2) Study how it is being done now
    (3) Question the present method
    (4) Determine actions to be taken
    (5) Chart proposed method
    (6) Get approval and apply
    (7) Solicit worker participation

12. *CORRECTIVE TECHNIQUES OF JOB IMPROVEMENT*

Specific Problems	General Improvement	Corrective Techniques
(1) Size of workload	(1) Departmental layout	(1) Study with scale model
(2) Inability to meet schedules	(2) Flow of work	(2) Flow chart study
(3) Strain and fatigue	(3) Work plan layout	(3) Motion analysis
(4) Improper use of men and skills	(4) Utilization of manpower	(4) Comparison of units produced to standard allowance
(5) Waste, poor quality, unsafe conditions	(5) Work methods	(5) Methods analysis
(6) Bottleneck conditions that hinder output	(6) Materials handling	(6) Flow chart & equipment study
(7) Poor utilization of equipment and machine	(7) Utilization of equipment	(7) Down time vs. running time
(8) Efficiency and productivity of labor	(8) Motion economy	(8) Motion analysis

13. A *PLANNING CHECKLIST*

(1) Objectives
(2) Controls
(3) Delegations
(4) Communications
(5) Resources
(6) Resources
(7) Manpower
(8) Equipment
(9) Supplies and materials
(10) Utilization of time
(11) Safety
(12) Money
(13) Work
(14) Timing of improvements

14. *FIVE CHARACTERISTICS OF GOOD DIRECTIONS*

In order to get results, directions must be:

(1) Possible of accomplishment
(2) Agreeable with worker interests
(3) Related to mission
(4) Planned and complete
(5) Unmistakably clear

15. *TYPES OF DIRECTIONS*

(1) Demands or direct orders
(2) Requests
(3) Suggestion or implication
(4) Volunteering

16. *CONTROLS*

A typical listing of the overall areas in which the supervisor should establish controls might be:

(1) Manpower
(2) Materials
(3) Quality of work
(4) Quantity of work
(5) Time
(6) Space
(7) Money
(8) Methods

17. *ORIENTING THE NEW EMPLOYEE*

(1) Prepare for him
(2) Welcome the new employee
(3) Orientation for the job
(4) Follow-up

18. *CHECKLIST FOR ORIENTING NEW EMPLOYEES*

	Yes	No
(1) Do your appreciate the feelings of new employees when they first report for work?	___	___
(2) Are you aware of the fact that the new employee must make a big adjustment to his job?	___	___
(3) Have you given him good reasons for liking the job and the organization?	___	___
(4) Have you prepared for his first day on the job?		
(5) Did you welcome him cordially and make him feel needed?		
(6) Did you establish rapport with him so that he feels free to talk and discuss matters with you?	___	___
(7) Did you explain his job to him and his relationship to you?	___	___
(8) Does he know that his work will be evaluated periodically on a basis that is fair and objective?	___	___
(9) Did you introduce him to his fellow workers in such a way that they are likely to accept him?	___	___
(10) Does he know what employee benefits he will receive?		
(11) Does he understand the importance of being on the job and what to do if he must leave his duty station?	___	___
(12) Has he been impressed with the importance of accident prevention and safe practice?	___	___
(13) Does he generally know his way around the department?	___	___
(14) Is he under the guidance of a sponsor who will teach the right ways of doing things?	___	___
(15) Do you plan to follow-up so that he will continue to adjust successfully to his job?	___	___

19. *PRINCIPLES OF LEARNING*
    (1) Motivation (2) Demonstration or explanation (3) Practice

20. *CAUSES OF POOR PERFORMANCE*
    (1) Improper training for job
    (2) Wrong tools
    (3) Inadequate directions
    (4) Lack of supervisory follow-up
    (5) Poor communications
    (6) Lack of standards of performance
    (7) Wrong work habits
    (8) Low morale
    (9) Other

21. *FOUR MAJOR STEPS IN ON-THE-JOB INSTRUCTION*
    (1) Prepare the worker
    (2) Present the operation
    (3) Tryout performance
    (4) Follow-up

22. *EMPLOYEES WANT FIVE THINGS*
    (1) Security (2) Opportunity (3) Recognition (4) Inclusion (5) Expression

23. *SOME DON'TS IN REGARD TO PRAISE*
    (1) Don't praise a person for something he hasn't done
    (2) Don't praise a person unless you can be sincere
    (3) Don't be sparing in praise just because your superior withholds it from you
    (4) Don't let too much time elapse between good performance and recognition of it

24. *HOW TO GAIN YOUR WORKERS' CONFIDENCE*
    Methods of developing confidence include such things as:
    (1) Knowing the interests, habits, hobbies of employees
    (2) Admitting your own inadequacies
    (3) Sharing and telling of confidence in others
    (4) Supporting people when they are in trouble
    (5) Delegating matters that can be well handled
    (6) Being frank and straightforward about problems and working conditions
    (7) Encouraging others to bring their problems to you
    (8) Taking action on problems which impede worker progress

25. *SOURCES OF EMPLOYEE PROBLEMS*
    On-the-job causes might be such things as:
    (1) A feeling that favoritism is exercised in assignments
    (2) Assignment of overtime
    (3) An undue amount of supervision
    (4) Changing methods or systems
    (5) Stealing of ideas or trade secrets
    (6) Lack of interest in job
    (7) Threat of reduction in force
    (8) Ignorance or lack of communications
    (9) Poor equipment
    (10) Lack of knowing how supervisor feels toward employee
    (11) Shift assignments

    Off-the-job problems might have to do with:
    (1) Health (2) Finances (3) Housing (4) Family

26. *THE SUPERVISOR'S KEY TO DISCIPLINE*

There are several key points about discipline which the supervisor should keep in mind:

(1) Job discipline is one of the disciplines of life and is directed by the supervisor.
(2) It is more important to correct an employee fault than to fix blame for it.
(3) Employee performance is affected by problems both on the job and off.
(4) Sudden or abrupt changes in behavior can be indications of important employee problems.
(5) Problems should be dealt with as soon as possible after they are identified.
(6) The attitude of the supervisor may have more to do with solving problems than the techniques of problem solving.
(7) Correction of employee behavior should be resorted to only after the supervisor is sure that training or counseling will not be helpful.
(8) Be sure to document your disciplinary actions.
(9) Make sure that you are disciplining on the basis of facts rather than personal feelings.
(10) Take each disciplinary step in order, being careful not to make snap judgments, or decisions based on impatience.

27. *FIVE IMPORTANT PROCESSES OF MANAGEMENT*

(1) Planning
(2) Organizing
(3) Scheduling
(4) Controlling
(5) Motivating

28. *WHEN THE SUPERVISOR FAILS TO PLAN*

(1) Supervisor creates impression of not knowing his job
(2) May lead to excessive overtime
(3) Job runs itself -- supervisor lacks control
(4) Deadlines and appointments missed
(5) Parts of the work go undone
(6) Work interrupted by emergencies
(7) Sets a bad example
(8) Uneven workload creates peaks and valleys
(9) Too much time on minor details at expense of more important tasks

29. *FOURTEEN GENERAL PRINCIPLES OF MANAGEMENT*

(1) Division of work
(2) Authority and responsibility
(3) Discipline
(4) Unity of command
(5) Unity of direction
(6) Subordination of individual interest to general interest
(7) Remuneration of personnel
(8) Centralization
(9) Scalar chain
(10) Order
(11) Equity
(12) Stability of tenure of personnel
(13) Initiative
(14) Esprit de corps

30. *CHANGE*

Bringing about change is perhaps attempted more often, and yet less well understood, than anything else the supervisor does. How do people generally react to change? (People tend to resist change that is imposed upon them by other individuals or circumstances.

Change is characteristic of every situation. It is a part of every real endeavor where the efforts of people are concerned.

A. Why do people resist change?
People may resist change because of:
(1) Fear of the unknown
(2) Implied criticism
(3) Unpleasant experiences in the past
(4) Fear of loss of status
(5) Threat to the ego
(6) Fear of loss of economic stability

B. How can we best overcome the resistance to change?
In initiating change, take these steps:
(1) Get ready to sell
(2) Identify sources of help
(3) Anticipate objections
(4) Sell benefits
(5) Listen in depth
(6) Follow up

B. BRIEF TOPICAL SUMMARIES

I. WHO/WHAT IS THE SUPERVISOR?

1. The supervisor is often called the "highest level employee and the lowest level manager."
2. A supervisor is a member of both management and the work group. He acts as a bridge between the two.
3. Most problems in supervision are in the area of human relations, or people problems.
4. Employees expect: Respect, opportunity to learn and to advance, and a sense of belonging, and so forth.
5. Supervisors are responsible for directing people and organizing work. Planning is of paramount importance.
6. A position description is a set of duties and responsibilities inherent to a given position.
7. It is important to keep the position description up-to-date and to provide each employee with his own copy.

II. THE SOCIOLOGY OF WORK

1. People are alike in many ways; however, each individual is unique.
2. The supervisor is challenged in getting to know employee differences. Acquiring skills in evaluating individuals is an asset.
3. Maintaining meaningful working relationships in the organization is of great importance.
4. The supervisor has an obligation to help individuals to develop to their fullest potential.
5. Job rotation on a planned basis helps to build versatility and to maintain interest and enthusiasm in work groups.
6. Cross training (job rotation) provides backup skills.
7. The supervisor can help reduce tension by maintaining a sense of humor, providing guidance to employees, and by making reasonable and timely decisions. Employees respond favorably to working under reasonably predictable circumstances.
8. Change is characteristic of all managerial behavior. The supervisor must adjust to changes in procedures, new methods, technological changes, and to a number of new and sometimes challenging situations.
9. To overcome the natural tendency for people to resist change, the supervisor should become more skillful in initiating change.

III. PRINCIPLES AND PRACTICES OF SUPERVISION

1. Employees should be required to answer to only one superior.
2. A supervisor can effectively direct only a limited number of employees, depending upon the complexity, variety, and proximity of the jobs involved.
3. The organizational chart presents the organization in graphic form. It reflects lines of authority and responsibility as well as interrelationships of units within the organization.
4. Distribution of work can be improved through an analysis using the "Work Distribution Chart."
5. The "Work Distribution Chart" reflects the division of work within a unit in understandable form.
6. When related tasks are given to an employee, he has a better chance of increasing his skills through training.
7. The individual who is given the responsibility for tasks must also be given the appropriate authority to insure adequate results.
8. The supervisor should delegate repetitive, routine work. Preparation of recurring reports, maintaining leave and attendance records are some examples.
9. Good discipline is essential to good task performance. Discipline is reflected in the actions of employees on the job in the absence of supervision.
10. Disciplinary action may have to be taken when the positive aspects of discipline have failed. Reprimand, warning, and suspension are examples of disciplinary action.
11. If a situation calls for a reprimand, be sure it is deserved and remember it is to be done in private.

IV. DYNAMIC LEADERSHIP

1. A style is a personal method or manner of exerting influence.
2. Authoritarian leaders often see themselves as the source of power and authority.
3. The democratic leader often perceives the group as the source of authority and power.
4. Supervisors tend to do better when using the pattern of leadership that is most natural for them.
5. Social scientists suggest that the effective supervisor use the leadership style that best fits the problem or circumstances involved.
6. All four styles -- telling, selling, consulting, joining -- have their place. Using one does not preclude using the other at another time.
7. The theory X point of view assumes that the average person dislikes work, will avoid it whenever possible, and must be coerced to achieve organizational objectives.
8. The theory Y point of view assumes that the average person considers work to be as natural as play, and, when the individual is committed, he requires little supervision or direction to accomplish desired objectives.
9. The leader's basic assumptions concerning human behavior and human nature affect his actions, decisions, and other managerial practices.
10. Dissatisfaction among employees is often present, but difficult to isolate. The supervisor should seek to weaken dissatisfaction by keeping promises, being sincere and considerate, keeping employees informed, and so forth.
11. Constructive suggestions should be encouraged during the natural progress of the work.

V. PROCESSES FOR SOLVING PROBLEMS

1. People find their daily tasks more meaningful and satisfying when they can improve them.
2. The causes of problems, or the key factors, are often hidden in the background. Ability to solve problems often involves the ability to isolate them from their backgrounds. There is some substance to the cliché that some persons "can't see the forest for the trees."
3. New procedures are often developed from old ones. Problems should be broken down into manageable parts. New ideas can be adapted from old ones.

4. People think differently in problem-solving situations. Using a logical, patterned approach is often useful. One approach found to be useful includes these steps:
   (a) Define the problem
   (b) Establish objectives
   (c) Get the facts
   (d) Weigh and decide
   (e) Take action
   (f) Evaluate action

VI. TRAINING FOR RESULTS

1. Participants respond best when they feel training is important to them.
2. The supervisor has responsibility for the training and development of those who report to him.
3. When training is delegated to others, great care must be exercised to insure the trainer has knowledge, aptitude, and interest for his work as a trainer.
4. Training (learning) of some type goes on continually. The most successful supervisor makes certain the learning contributes in a productive manner to operational goals.
5. New employees are particularly susceptible to training. Older employees facing new job situations require specific training, as well as having need for development and growth opportunities.
6. Training needs require continuous monitoring.
7. The training officer of an agency is a professional with a responsibility to assist supervisors in solving training problems.
8. Many of the self-development steps important to the supervisor's own growth are equally important to the development of peers and subordinates. Knowledge of these is important when the supervisor consults with others on development and growth opportunities.

VII. HEALTH, SAFETY, AND ACCIDENT PREVENTION

1. Management-minded supervisors take appropriate measures to assist employees in maintaining health and in assuring safe practices in the work environment.
2. Effective safety training and practices help to avoid injury and accidents.
3. Safety should be a management goal. All infractions of safety which are observed should be corrected without exception.
4. Employees' safety attitude, training and instruction, provision of safe tools and equipment, supervision, and leadership are considered highly important factors which contribute to safety and which can be influenced directly by supervisors.
5. When accidents do occur they should be investigated promptly for very important reasons, including the fact that information which is gained can be used to prevent accidents in the future.

VIII. EQUAL EMPLOYMENT OPPORTUNITY

1. The supervisor should endeavor to treat all employees fairly, without regard to religion, race, sex, or national origin.
2. Groups tend to reflect the attitude of the leader. Prejudice can be detected even in very subtle form. Supervisors must strive to create a feeling of mutual respect and confidence in every employee.
3. Complete utilization of all human resources is a national goal. Equitable consideration should be accorded women in the work force, minority-group members, the physically and mentally handicapped, and the older employee. The important question is: "Who can do the job?"
4. Training opportunities, recognition for performance, overtime assignments, promotional opportunities, and all other personnel actions are to be handled on an equitable basis.

IX. IMPROVING COMMUNICATIONS

1. Communications is achieving understanding between the sender and the receiver of a message. It also means sharing information -- the creation of understanding.
2. Communication is basic to all human activity. Words are means of conveying meanings; however, real meanings are in people.
3. There are very practical differences in the effectiveness of one-way, impersonal, and two-way communications. Words spoken face-to-face are better understood. Telephone conversations are effective, but lack the rapport of person-to-person exchanges. The whole person communicates.
4. Cooperation and communication in an organization go hand in hand. When there is a mutual respect between people, spelling out rules and procedures for communicating is unnecessary.
5. There are several barriers to effective communications. These include failure to listen with respect and understanding, lack of skill in feedback, and misinterpreting the meanings of words used by the speaker. It is also common practice to listen to what we want to hear, and tune out things we do not want to hear.
6. Communication is management's chief problem. The supervisor should accept the challenge to communicate more effectively and to improve interagency and intra-agency communications.
7. The supervisor may often plan for and conduct meetings. The planning phase is critical and may determine the success or the failure of a meeting.
8. Speaking before groups usually requires extra effort. Stage fright may never disappear completely, but it can be controlled.

X. SELF-DEVELOPMENT

1. Every employee is responsible for his own self-development.
2. Toastmaster and toastmistress clubs offer opportunities to improve skills in oral communications.
3. Planning for one's own self-development is of vital importance. Supervisors know their own strengths and limitations better than anyone else.
4. Many opportunities are open to aid the supervisor in his developmental efforts, including job assignments; training opportunities, both governmental and non-governmental -- to include universities and professional conferences and seminars.
5. Programmed instruction offers a means of studying at one's own rate.
6. Where difficulties may arise from a supervisor's being away from his work for training, he may participate in televised home study or correspondence courses to meet his self-develop- ment needs.

XI. TEACHING AND TRAINING

A. The Teaching Process

Teaching is encouraging and guiding the learning activities of students toward established goals. In most cases this process consists in five steps: preparation, presentation, summarization, evaluation, and application.

1. Preparation

Preparation is twofold in nature; that of the supervisor and the employee.

Preparation by the supervisor is absolutely essential to success. He must know what, when, where, how, and whom he will teach. Some of the factors that should be considered are:

(1) The objectives
(2) The materials needed
(3) The methods to be used
(4) Employee participation
(5) Employee interest
(6) Training aids
(7) Evaluation
(8) Summarization

Employee preparation consists in preparing the employee to receive the material. Probably the most important single factor in the preparation of the employee is arousing and maintaining his interest. He must know the objectives of the training, why he is there, how the material can be used, and its importance to him.

2. Presentation

In presentation, have a carefully designed plan and follow it. The plan should be accurate and complete, yet flexible enough to meet situations as they arise. The method of presentation will be determined by the particular situation and objectives.

3. Summary

A summary should be made at the end of every training unit and program. In addition, there may be internal summaries depending on the nature of the material being taught. The important thing is that the trainee must always be able to understand how each part of the new material relates to the whole.

4. Application

The supervisor must arrange work so the employee will be given a chance to apply new knowledge or skills while the material is still clear in his mind and interest is high. The trainee does not really know whether he has learned the material until he has been given a chance to apply it. If the material is not applied, it loses most of its value.

5. Evaluation

The purpose of all training is to promote learning. To determine whether the training has been a success or failure, the supervisor must evaluate this learning.

In the broadest sense evaluation includes all the devices, methods, skills, and techniques used by the supervisor to keep him self and the employees informed as to their progress toward the objectives they are pursuing. The extent to which the employee has mastered the knowledge, skills, and abilities, or changed his attitudes, as determined by the program objectives, is the extent to which instruction has succeeded or failed.

Evaluation should not be confined to the end of the lesson, day, or program but should be used continuously. We shall note later the way this relates to the rest of the teaching process.

B. Teaching Methods

A teaching method is a pattern of identifiable student and instructor activity used in presenting training material.

All supervisors are faced with the problem of deciding which method should be used at a given time.

As with all methods, there are certain advantages and disadvantages to each method.

1. Lecture

The lecture is direct oral presentation of material by the supervisor. The present trend is to place less emphasis on the trainer's activity and more on that of the trainee.

2. Discussion

Teaching by discussion or conference involves using questions and other techniques to arouse interest and focus attention upon certain areas, and by doing so creating a learning situation. This can be one of the most valuable methods because it gives the employees 'an opportunity to express their ideas and pool their knowledge.

3. Demonstration

The demonstration is used to teach how something works or how to do something. It can be used to show a principle or what the results of a series of actions will be. A well-staged demonstration is particularly effective because it shows proper methods of performance in a realistic manner.

4. Performance

Performance is one of the most fundamental of all learning techniques or teaching methods. The trainee may be able to tell how a specific operation should be performed but he cannot be sure he knows how to perform the operation until he has done so.

5. Which Method to Use

Moreover, there are other methods and techniques of teaching. It is difficult to use any method without other methods entering into it. In any learning situation a combination of methods is usually more effective than anyone method alone.

Finally, evaluation must be integrated into the other aspects of the teaching-learning process.

It must be used in the motivation of the trainees; it must be used to assist in developing understanding during the training; and it must be related to employee application of the results of training.

This is distinctly the role of the supervisor.

GLOSSARY OF LEGAL TERMS

TABLE OF CONTENTS

GLOSSARY OF LEGAL TERMS

A

ACTION - "Action" includes a civil action and a criminal action.
A FORTIORI - A term meaning you can reason one thing from the existence of certain facts.
A POSTERIORI - From what goes after; from effect to cause.
A PRIORI - From what goes before; from cause to effect.
AB INITIO - From the beginning.
ABATE - To diminish or put an end to.
ABET - To encourage the commission of a crime.
ABEYANCE - Suspension, temporary suppression.
ABIDE - To accept the consequences of.
ABJURE - To renounce; give up.
ABRIDGE - To reduce; contract; diminish.
ABROGATE - To annul, repeal, or destroy.
ABSCOND - To hide or absent oneself to avoid legal action.
ABSTRACT - A summary.
ABUT - To border on, to touch.
ACCESS - Approach; in real property law it means the right of the owner of property to the use of the highway or road next to his land, without obstruction by intervening property owners.
ACCESSORY - In criminal law, it means the person who contributes or aids in the commission of a crime.
ACCOMMODATED PARTY - One to whom credit is extended on the strength of another person signing a commercial paper.
ACCOMMODATION PAPER - A commercial paper to which the accommodating party has put his name.
ACCOMPLICE - In criminal law, it means a person who together with the principal offender commits a crime.
ACCORD - An agreement to accept something different or less than that to which one is entitled, which extinguishes the entire obligation.
ACCOUNT - A statement of mutual demands in the nature of debt and credit between parties.
ACCRETION - The act of adding to a thing; in real property law, it means gradual accumulation of land by natural causes.
ACCRUE - To grow to; to be added to.
ACKNOWLEDGMENT - The act of going before an official authorized to take acknowledgments, and acknowledging an act as one's own.
ACQUIESCENCE - A silent appearance of consent.
ACQUIT - To legally determine the innocence of one charged with a crime.
AD INFINITUM - Indefinitely.
AD LITEM - For the suit.
AD VALOREM - According to value.
ADJECTIVE LAW - Rules of procedure.
ADJUDICATION - The judgment given in a case.
ADMIRALTY - Court having jurisdiction over maritime cases.
ADULT - Sixteen years old or over (in criminal law).
ADVANCE - In commercial law, it means to pay money or render other value before it is due.
ADVERSE - Opposed; contrary.
ADVOCATE - (v.) To speak in favor of;
(n.) One who assists, defends, or pleads for another.
AFFIANT - A person who makes and signs an affidavit.

AFFIDAVIT - A written and sworn to declaration of facts, voluntarily made.
AFFINITY- The relationship between persons through marriage with the kindred of each other; distinguished from consanguinity, which is the relationship by blood.
AFFIRM - To ratify; also when an appellate court affirms a judgment, decree, or order, it means that it is valid and right and must stand as rendered in the lower court.
AFOREMENTIONED; AFORESAID - Before or already said.
AGENT - One who represents and acts for another.
AID AND COMFORT - To help; encourage.
ALIAS - A name not one's true name.
ALIBI - A claim of not being present at a certain place at a certain time.
ALLEGE - To assert.
ALLOTMENT - A share or portion.
AMBIGUITY - Uncertainty; capable of being understood in more than one way.
AMENDMENT - Any language made or proposed as a change in some principal writing.
AMICUS CURIAE - A friend of the court; one who has an interest in a case, although not a party in the case, who volunteers advice upon matters of law to the judge. For example, a brief amicus curiae.
AMORTIZATION - To provide for a gradual extinction of (a future obligation) in advance of maturity, especially, by periodical contributions to a sinking fund which will be adequate to discharge a debt or make a replacement when it becomes necessary.
ANCILLARY - Aiding, auxiliary.
ANNOTATION - A note added by way of comment or explanation.
ANSWER - A written statement made by a defendant setting forth the grounds of his defense.
ANTE - Before.
ANTE MORTEM - Before death.
APPEAL - The removal of a case from a lower court to one of superior jurisdiction for the purpose of obtaining a review.
APPEARANCE - Coming into court as a party to a suit.
APPELLANT - The party who takes an appeal from one court or jurisdiction to another (appellate) court for review.
APPELLEE - The party against whom an appeal is taken.
APPROPRIATE - To make a thing one's own.
APPROPRIATION - Prescribing the destination of a thing; the act of the legislature designating a particular fund, to be applied to some object of government expenditure.
APPURTENANT - Belonging to; accessory or incident to.
ARBITER - One who decides a dispute; a referee.
ARBITRARY - Unreasoned; not governed by any fixed rules or standard.
ARGUENDO - By way of argument.
ARRAIGN - To call the prisoner before the court to answer to a charge.
ASSENT - A declaration of willingness to do something in compliance with a request.
ASSERT - Declare.
ASSESS - To fix the rate or amount.
ASSIGN - To transfer; to appoint; to select for a particular purpose.
ASSIGNEE - One who receives an assignment.
ASSIGNOR - One who makes an assignment.
AT BAR - Before the court.

AT ISSUE - When parties in an action come to a point where one asserts something and the other denies it.
ATTACH - Seize property by court order and sometimes arrest a person.
ATTEST - To witness a will, etc.; act of attestation.
AVERMENT - A positive statement of facts.

B

BAIL - To obtain the release of a person from legal custody by giving security and promising that he shall appear in court; to deliver (goods, etc.) in trust to a person for a special purpose.
BAILEE - One to whom personal property is delivered under a contract of bailment.
BAILMENT - Delivery of personal property to another to be held for a certain purpose and to be returned when the purpose is accomplished.
BAILOR - The party who delivers goods to another, under a contract of bailment.
BANC (OR BANK) - Bench; the place where a court sits permanently or regularly; also the assembly of all the judges of a court.
BANKRUPT - An insolvent person, technically, one declared to be bankrupt after a bankruptcy proceeding.
BAR - The legal profession.
BARRATRY - Exciting groundless judicial proceedings.
BARTER - A contract by which parties exchange goods for other goods.
BATTERY - Illegal interfering with another's person.
BEARER - In commercial law, it means the person in possession of a commercial paper which is payable to the bearer.
BENCH - The court itself or the judge.
BENEFICIARY - A person benefiting under a will, trust, or agreement.
BEST EVIDENCE RULE,THE - Except as otherwise provided by statute, no evidence other than the writing itself is admissible to prove the content of a writing. This section shall be known and may be cited as the best evidence rule.
BEQUEST - A gift of personal property under a will.
BILL - A formal written statement of complaint to a court of justice; also, a draft of an act of the legislature before it becomes a law; also, accounts for goods sold, services rendered, or work done.
BONA FIDE - In or with good faith; honestly.
BOND - An instrument by which the maker promises to pay a sum of money to another, usually providing that upon performances of a certain condition the obligation shall be void.
BOYCOTT - A plan to prevent the carrying on of a business by wrongful means.
BREACH - The breaking or violating of a law, or the failure to carry out a duty.
BRIEF - A written document, prepared by a lawyer to serve as the basis of an argument upon a case in court, usually an appellate court.
BURDEN OF PRODUCING EVIDENCE - The obligation of a party to introduce evidence sufficient to avoid a ruling against him on the issue.
BURDEN OF PROOF - The obligation of a party to establish by evidence a requisite degree of belief concerning a fact in the mind of the trier of fact or the court. The burden of proof may require a party to raise a reasonable doubt concerning the existence of nonexistence of a fact or that he establish the existence or nonexistence of a fact by a preponderance of the evidence, by clear and convincing proof, or by proof beyond a reasonable doubt.

Except as otherwise provided by law, the burden of proof requires proof by a preponderance of the evidence.

BUSINESS, A - Shall include every kind of business, profession, occupation, calling or operation of institutions, whether carried on for profit or not.
BY-LAWS - Regulations, ordinances, or rules enacted by a corporation, association, etc., for its own government.

C

CANON - A doctrine; also, a law or rule, of a church or association in particular.
CAPIAS - An order to arrest.
CAPTION - In a pleading, deposition or other paper connected with a case in court, it is the heading or introductory clause which shows the names of the parties, name of the court, number of the case on the docket or calendar, etc.
CARRIER - A person or corporation undertaking to transport persons or property.
CASE - A general term for an action, cause, suit, or controversy before a judicial body.
CAUSE - A suit, litigation or action before a court.
CAVEAT EMPTOR - Let the buyer beware. This term expresses the rule that the purchaser of an article must examine, judge, and test it for himself, being bound to discover any obvious defects or imperfections.
CERTIFICATE - A written representation that some legal formality has been complied with.
CERTIORARI - To be informed of; the name of a writ issued by a superior court directing the lower court to send up to the former the record and proceedings of a case.
CHANGE OF VENUE - To remove place of trial from one place to another.
CHARGE - An obligation or duty; a formal complaint; an instruction of the court to the jury upon a case.
CHARTER - (n.) The authority by virtue of which an organized body acts;
(v.) in mercantile law, it means to hire or lease a vehicle or vessel for transportation.
CHATTEL - An article of personal property.
CHATTEL MORTGAGE - A mortgage on personal property.
CIRCUIT - A division of the country, for the administration of justice; a geographical area served by a court.
CITATION - The act of the court by which a person is summoned or cited; also, a reference to legal authority.
CIVIL (ACTIONS)- It indicates the private rights and remedies of individuals in contrast to the word "criminal" (actions) which relates to prosecution for violation of laws.
CLAIM (n.) - Any demand held or asserted as of right.
CODICIL - An addition to a will.
CODIFY - To arrange the laws of a country into a code.
COGNIZANCE - Notice or knowledge.
COLLATERAL - By the side; accompanying; an article or thing given to secure performance of a promise.
COMITY - Courtesy; the practice by which one court follows the decision of another court on the same question.
COMMIT - To perform, as an act; to perpetrate, as a crime; to send a person to prison.
COMMON LAW - As distinguished from law created by the enactment of the legislature (called statutory law), it relates to those principles and rules of action which derive their authority solely from usages and customs of immemorial antiquity, particularly with reference to the ancient unwritten law of England. The written pronouncements of the common law are found in court decisions.
COMMUTE - Change punishment to one less severe.

COMPLAINANT - One who applies to the court for legal redress.
COMPLAINT - The pleading of a plaintiff in a civil action; or a charge that a person has committed a specified offense.
COMPROMISE - An arrangement for settling a dispute by agreement.
CONCUR - To agree, consent.
CONCURRENT - Running together, at the same time.
CONDEMNATION - Taking private property for public use on payment therefor.
CONDITION - Mode or state of being; a qualification or restriction.
CONDUCT - Active and passive behavior; both verbal and nonverbal.
CONFESSION - Voluntary statement of guilt of crime.
CONFIDENTIAL COMMUNICATION BETWEEN CLIENT AND LAWYER - Information transmitted between a client and his lawyer in the course of that relationship and in confidence by a means which, so far as the client is aware, discloses the information to no third persons other than those who are present to further the interest of the client in the consultation or those to whom disclosure is reasonably necessary for the transmission of the information or the accomplishment of the purpose for which the lawyer is consulted, and includes a legal opinion formed and the advice given by the lawyer in the course of that relationship.
CONFRONTATION - Witness testifying in presence of defendant.
CONSANGUINITY - Blood relationship.
CONSIGN - To give in charge; commit; entrust; to send or transmit goods to a merchant, factor, or agent for sale.
CONSIGNEE - One to whom a consignment is made.
CONSIGNOR - One who sends or makes a consignment.
CONSPIRACY - In criminal law, it means an agreement between two or more persons to commit an unlawful act.
CONSPIRATORS - Persons involved in a conspiracy.
CONSTITUTION - The fundamental law of a nation or state.
CONSTRUCTION OF GENDERS - The masculine gender includes the feminine and neuter.
CONSTRUCTION OF SINGULAR AND PLURAL - The singular number includes the plural; and the plural, the singular.
CONSTRUCTION OF TENSES - The present tense includes the past and future tenses; and the future, the present.
CONSTRUCTIVE - An act or condition assumed from other parts or conditions.
CONSTRUE - To ascertain the meaning of language.
CONSUMMATE - To complete.
CONTIGUOUS - Adjoining; touching; bounded by.
CONTINGENT - Possible, but not assured; dependent upon some condition.
CONTINUANCE - The adjournment or postponement of an action pending in a court.
CONTRA - Against, opposed to; contrary.
CONTRACT - An agreement between two or more persons to do or not to do a particular thing.
CONTROVERT - To dispute, deny.
CONVERSION - Dealing with the personal property of another as if it were one's own, without right.
CONVEYANCE - An instrument transferring title to land.
CONVICTION - Generally, the result of a criminal trial which ends in a judgment or sentence that the defendant is guilty as charged.

COOPERATIVE - A cooperative is a voluntary organization of persons with a common interest, formed and operated along democratic lines for the purpose of supplying services at cost to its members and other patrons, who contribute both capital and business.
CORPUS DELICTI - The body of a crime; the crime itself.
CORROBORATE - To strengthen; to add weight by additional evidence.
COUNTERCLAIM - A claim presented by a defendant in opposition to or deduction from the claim of the plaintiff.
COUNTY - Political subdivision of a state.
COVENANT - Agreement.
CREDIBLE - Worthy of belief.
CREDITOR - A person to whom a debt is owing by another person, called the "debtor."
CRIMINAL ACTION - Includes criminal proceedings.
CRIMINAL INFORMATION - Same as complaint.
CRITERION (sing.)
CRITERIA (plural) - A means or tests for judging; a standard or standards.
CROSS-EXAMINATION - Examination of a witness by a party other than the direct examiner upon a matter that is within the scope of the direct examination of the witness.
CULPABLE - Blamable.
CY-PRES - As near as (possible). The rule of *cy-pres* is a rule for the construction of instruments in equity by which the intention of the party is carried out *as near as may be*, when it would be impossible or illegal to give it literal effect.

D

DAMAGES - A monetary compensation, which may be recovered in the courts by any person who has suffered loss, or injury, whether to his person, property or rights through the unlawful act or omission or negligence of another.
DECLARANT - A person who makes a statement.
DE FACTO - In fact; actually but without legal authority.
DE JURE - Of right; legitimate; lawful.
DE MINIMIS - Very small or trifling.
DE NOVO - Anew; afresh; a second time.
DEBT - A specified sum of money owing to one person from another, including not only the obligation of the debtor to pay, but the right of the creditor to receive and enforce payment.
DECEDENT - A dead person.
DECISION - A judgment or decree pronounced by a court in determination of a case.
DECREE - An order of the court, determining the rights of all parties to a suit.
DEED - A writing containing a contract sealed and delivered; particularly to convey real property.
DEFALCATION - Misappropriation of funds.
DEFAMATION - Injuring one's reputation by false statements.
DEFAULT - The failure to fulfill a duty, observe a promise, discharge an obligation, or perform an agreement.
DEFENDANT - The person defending or denying; the party against whom relief or recovery is sought in an action or suit.
DEFRAUD - To practice fraud; to cheat or trick.
DELEGATE (v.)- To entrust to the care or management of another.
DELICTUS - A crime.
DEMUR (v.) - To dispute the sufficiency in law of the pleading of the other side.

DEMURRAGE - In maritime law, it means, the sum fixed or allowed as remuneration to the owners of a ship for the detention of their vessel beyond the number of days allowed for loading and unloading or for sailing; also used in railroad terminology.
DENIAL - A form of pleading; refusing to admit the truth of a statement, charge, etc.
DEPONENT - One who gives testimony under oath reduced to writing.
DEPOSITION - Testimony given under oath outside of court for use in court or for the purpose of obtaining information in preparation for trial of a case.
DETERIORATION - A degeneration such as from decay, corrosion or disintegration.
DETRIMENT - Any loss or harm to person or property.
DEVIATION - A turning aside.
DEVISE - A gift of real property by the last will and testament of the donor.
DICTUM (sing.)
DICTA (plural) - Any statements made by the court in an opinion concerning some rule of law not necessarily involved nor essential to the determination of the case.
DIRECT EVIDENCE - Evidence that directly proves a fact, without an inference or presumption, and which in itself if true, conclusively establishes that fact.
DIRECT EXAMINATION - The first examination of a witness upon a matter that is not within the scope of a previous examination of the witness.
DISAFFIRM - To repudiate.
DISMISS - In an action or suit, it means to dispose of the case without any further consideration or hearing.
DISSENT - To denote disagreement of one or more judges of a court with the decision passed by the majority upon a case before them.
DOCKET (n.) - A formal record, entered in brief, of the proceedings in a court.
DOCTRINE - A rule, principle, theory of law.
DOMICILE - That place where a man has his true, fixed and permanent home to which whenever he is absent he has the intention of returning.
DRAFT (n.) - A commercial paper ordering payment of money drawn by one person on another.
DRAWEE - The person who is requested to pay the money.
DRAWER - The person who draws the commercial paper and addresses it to the drawee.
DUPLICATE - A counterpart produced by the same impression as the original enlargements and miniatures, or by mechanical or electronic re-recording, or by chemical reproduction, or by other equivalent technique which accurately reproduces the original.
DURESS - Use of force to compel performance or non-performance of an act.

E

EASEMENT - A liberty, privilege, or advantage without profit, in the lands of another.
EGRESS - Act or right of going out or leaving; emergence.
EIUSDEM GENERIS - Of the same kind, class or nature. A rule used in the construction of language in a legal document.
EMBEZZLEMENT - To steal; to appropriate fraudulently to one's own use property entrusted to one's care.
EMBRACERY - Unlawful attempt to influence jurors, etc., but not by offering value.
EMINENT DOMAIN - The right of a state to take private property for public use.
ENACT - To make into a law.
ENDORSEMENT - Act of writing one's name on the back of a note, bill or similar written instrument.

ENJOIN - To require a person, by writ of injunction from a court of equity, to perform or to abstain or desist from some act.
ENTIRETY - The whole; that which the law considers as one whole, and not capable of being divided into parts.
ENTRAPMENT - Inducing one to commit a crime so as to arrest him.
ENUMERATED - Mentioned specifically; designated.
ENURE - To operate or take effect.
EQUITY - In its broadest sense, this term denotes the spirit and the habit of fairness, justness, and right dealing which regulate the conduct of men.
ERROR - A mistake of law, or the false or irregular application of law as will nullify the judicial proceedings.
ESCROW - A deed, bond or other written engagement, delivered to a third person, to be delivered by him only upon the performance or fulfillment of some condition.
ESTATE - The interest which any one has in lands, or in any other subject of property.
ESTOP - To stop, bar, or impede.
ESTOPPEL - A rule of law which prevents a man from alleging or denying a fact, because of his own previous act.
ET AL. (alii) - And others.
ET SEQ. (sequential) - And the following.
ET UX. (uxor) - And wife.
EVIDENCE - Testimony, writings, material objects, or other things presented to the senses that are offered to prove the existence or non-existence of a fact.

Means from which inferences may be drawn as a basis of proof in duly constituted judicial or fact finding tribunals, and includes testimony in the form of opinion and hearsay.

EX CONTRACTU
EX DELICTO - In law, rights and causes of action are divided into two classes, those arising *ex contractu* (from a contract) and those arising *ex delicto* (from a delict or tort).
EX OFFICIO - From office; by virtue of the office.
EX PARTE - On one side only; by or for one.
EX POST FACTO - After the fact.
EX POST FACTO LAW - A law passed after an act was done which retroactively makes such act a crime.
EX REL. (relations) - Upon relation or information.
EXCEPTION - An objection upon a matter of law to a decision made, either before or after judgment by a court.
EXECUTOR (male)
EXECUTRIX (female) - A person who has been appointed by will to execute the will.
EXECUTORY - That which is yet to be executed or performed.
EXEMPT - To release from some liability to which others are subject.
EXONERATION - The removal of a burden, charge or duty.
EXTRADITION - Surrender of a fugitive from one nation to another.

F

F.A.S.- "Free alongside ship"; delivery at dock for ship named.
F.O.B.- "Free on board"; seller will deliver to car, truck, vessel, or other conveyance by which goods are to be transported, without expense or risk of loss to the buyer or consignee.
FABRICATE - To construct; to invent a false story.
FACSIMILE - An exact or accurate copy of an original instrument.

FACTOR - A commercial agent.
FEASANCE - The doing of an act.
FELONIOUS - Criminal, malicious.
FELONY - Generally, a criminal offense that may be punished by death or imprisonment for more than one year as differentiated from a misdemeanor.
FEME SOLE - A single woman.
FIDUCIARY - A person who is invested with rights and powers to be exercised for the benefit of another person.
FIERI FACIAS - A writ of execution commanding the sheriff to levy and collect the amount of a judgment from the goods and chattels of the judgment debtor.
FINDING OF FACT - Determination from proof or judicial notice of the existence of a fact. A ruling implies a supporting finding of fact; no separate or formal finding is required unless required by a statute of this state.
FISCAL - Relating to accounts or the management of revenue.
FORECLOSURE (sale) - A sale of mortgaged property to obtain satisfaction of the mortgage out of the sale proceeds.
FORFEITURE - A penalty, a fine.
FORGERY - Fabricating or producing falsely, counterfeited.
FORTUITOUS - Accidental.
FORUM - A court of justice; a place of jurisdiction.
FRAUD - Deception; trickery.
FREEHOLDER - One who owns real property.
FUNGIBLE - Of such kind or nature that one specimen or part may be used in the place of another.

G

GARNISHEE - Person garnished.
GARNISHMENT - A legal process to reach the money or effects of a defendant, in the possession or control of a third person.
GRAND JURY - Not less than 16, not more than 23 citizens of a county sworn to inquire into crimes committed or triable in the county.
GRANT - To agree to; convey, especially real property.
GRANTEE - The person to whom a grant is made.
GRANTOR - The person by whom a grant is made.
GRATUITOUS - Given without a return, compensation or consideration.
GRAVAMEN - The grievance complained of or the substantial cause of a criminal action.
GUARANTY (n.) - A promise to answer for the payment of some debt, or the performance of some duty, in case of the failure of another person, who, in the first instance, is liable for such payment or performance.
GUARDIAN - The person, committee, or other representative authorized by law to protect the person or estate or both of an incompetent (or of a *sui juris* person having a guardian) and to act for him in matters affecting his person or property or both. An incompetent is a person under disability imposed by law.
GUILTY - Establishment of the fact that one has committed a breach of conduct, especially, a violation of law.

H

HABEAS CORPUS - You have the body; the name given to a variety of writs, having for their object to bring a party before a court or judge for decision as to whether such person is being lawfully held prisoner.
HABENDUM - In conveyancing; it is the clause in a deed conveying land which defines the extent of ownership to be held by the grantee.
HEARING - A proceeding whereby the arguments of the interested parties are heared.
HEARSAY - A type of testimony given by a witness who relates, not what he knows personally, but what others have told hi, or what he has heard said by others.
HEARSAY RULE, THE - (a) "Hearsay evidence" is evidence of a statement that was made other than by a witness while testifying at the hearing and that is offered to prove the truth of the matter stated; (b) Except as provided by law, hearsay evidence is inadmissible; (c) This section shall be known and may be cited as the hearsay rule.
HEIR - Generally, one who inherits property, real or personal.
HOLDER OF THE PRIVILEGE - (a) The client when he has no guardian or conservator; (b) A guardian or conservator of the client when the client has a guardian or conservator; (c) The personal representative of the client if the client is dead; (d) A successor, assign, trustee in dissolution, or any similar representative of a firm, association, organization, partnership, business trust, corporation, or public entity that is no longer in existence.
HUNG JURY - One so divided that they can't agree on a verdict.
HUSBAND-WIFE PRIVILEGE - An accused in a criminal proceeding has a privilege to prevent his spouse from testifying against him.
HYPOTHECATE - To pledge a thing without delivering it to the pledgee.
HYPOTHESIS - A supposition, assumption, or toehry.

I

I.E. (id est) - That is.
IB., OR IBID.(ibidem) - In the same place; used to refer to a legal reference previously cited to avoid repeating the entire citation.
ILLICIT - Prohibited; unlawful.
ILLUSORY - Deceiving by false appearance.
IMMUNITY - Exemption.
IMPEACH - To accuse, to dispute.
IMPEDIMENTS - Disabilities, or hindrances.
IMPLEAD - To sue or prosecute by due course of law.
IMPUTED - Attributed or charged to.
IN LOCO PARENTIS - In place of parent, a guardian.
IN TOTO - In the whole; completely.
INCHOATE - Imperfect; unfinished.
INCOMMUNICADO - Denial of the right of a prisoner to communicate with friends or relatives.
INCOMPETENT - One who is incapable of caring for his own affairs because he is mentally deficient or undeveloped.
INCRIMINATION - A matter will incriminate a person if it constitutes, or forms an essential part of, or, taken in connection with other matters disclosed, is a basis for a reasonable inference of such a violation of the laws of this State as to subject him to liability to punishment therefor, unless he has become for any reason permanently immune from punishment for such violation.
INCUMBRANCE - Generally a claim, lien, charge or liability attached to and binding real property.

INDEMNIFY - To secure against loss or damage; also, to make reimbursement to one for a loss already incurred by him.
INDEMNITY - An agreement to reimburse another person in case of an anticipated loss falling upon him.
INDICIA - Signs; indications.
INDICTMENT - An accusation in writing found and presented by a grand jury charging that a person has committed a crime.
INDORSE - To write a name on the back of a legal paper or document, generally, a negotiable instrument
INDUCEMENT - Cause or reason why a thing is done or that which incites the person to do the act or commit a crime; the motive for the criminal act.
INFANT - In civil cases one under 21 years of age.
INFORMATION - A formal accusation of crime made by a prosecuting attorney.
INFRA - Below, under; this word occurring by itself in a publication refers the reader to a future part of the publication.
INGRESS - The act of going into.
INJUNCTION - A writ or order by the court requiring a person, generally, to do or to refrain from doing an act.
INSOLVENT - The condition of a person who is unable to pay his debts.
INSTRUCTION - A direction given by the judge to the jury concerning the law of the case.
INTERIM - In the meantime; time intervening.
INTERLOCUTORY - Temporary, not final; something intervening between the commencement and the end of a suit which decides some point or matter, but is not a final decision of the whole controversy.
INTERROGATORIES - A series of formal written questions used in the examination of a party or a witness usually prior to a trial.
INTESTATE - A person who dies without a will.
INURE - To result, to take effect.
IPSO FACTO - By the fact iself; by the mere fact.
ISSUE (n.) The disputed point or question in a case,

J

JEOPARDY - Danger, hazard, peril.
JOINDER - Joining; uniting with another person in some legal steps or proceeding.
JOINT - United; combined.
JUDGE - Member or members or representative or representatives of a court conducting a trial or hearing at which evidence is introduced.
JUDGMENT - The official decision of a court of justice.
JUDICIAL OR JUDICIARY - Relating to or connected with the administration of justice.
JURAT - The clause written at the foot of an affidavit, stating when, where and before whom such affidavit was sworn.
JURISDICTION - The authority to hear and determine controversies between parties.
JURISPRUDENCE - The philosophy of law.
JURY - A body of persons legally selected to inquire into any matter of fact, and to render their verdict according to the evidence.

L

LACHES - The failure to diligently assert a right, which results in a refusal to allow relief.

LANDLORD AND TENANT - A phrase used to denote the legal relation existing between the owner and occupant of real estate.
LARCENY - Stealing personal property belonging to another.
LATENT - Hidden; that which does not appear on the face of a thing.
LAW - Includes constitutional, statutory, and decisional law.
LAWYER-CLIENT PRIVILEGE - (1) A "client" is a person, public officer, or corporation, association, or other organization or entity, either public or private, who is rendered professional legal services by a lawyer, or who consults a lawyer with a view to obtaining professional legal services from him; (2) A "lawyer" is a person authorized, or reasonably believed by the client to be authorized, to practice law in any state or nation; (3) A "representative of the lawyer" is one employed to assist the lawyer in the rendition of professional legal services; (4) A communication is "confidential" if not intended to be disclosed to third persons other than those to whom disclosure is in furtherance of the rendition of professional legal services to the client or those reasonably necessary for the transmission of the communication.

General rule of privilege - A client has a privilege to refuse to disclose and to prevent any other person from disclosing confidential communications made for the purpose of facilitating the rendition of professional legal services to the client, (1) between himself or his representative and his lawyer or his lawyer's representative, or (2) between his lawyer and the lawyer's representative, or (3) by him or his lawyer to a lawyer representing another in a matter of common interest, or (4) between representatives of the client or between the client and a representative of the client, or (5) between lawyers representing the client.

LEADING QUESTION - Question that suggests to the witness the answer that the examining party desires.
LEASE - A contract by which one conveys real estate for a limited time usually for a specified rent; personal property also may be leased.
LEGISLATION - The act of enacting laws.
LEGITIMATE - Lawful.
LESSEE - One to whom a lease is given.
LESSOR - One who grants a lease
LEVY - A collecting or exacting by authority.
LIABLE - Responsible; bound or obligated in law or equity.
LIBEL (v.) - To defame or injure a person's reputation by a published writing.
(n.) - The initial pleading on the part of the plaintiff in an admiralty proceeding.
LIEN - A hold or claim which one person has upon the property of another as a security for some debt or charge.
LIQUIDATED - Fixed; settled.
LIS PENDENS - A pending civil or criminal action.
LITERAL - According to the language.
LITIGANT - A party to a lawsuit.
LITATION - A judicial controversy.
LOCUS - A place.
LOCUS DELICTI - Place of the crime.
LOCUS POENITENTIAE - The abandoning or giving up of one's intention to commit some crime before it is fully completed or abandoning a conspiracy before its purpose is accomplished.

M

MALFEASANCE - To do a wrongful act.
MALICE - The doing of a wrongful act Intentionally without just cause or excuse.

MANDAMUS - The name of a writ issued by a court to enforce the performance of some public duty.
MANDATORY (adj.) Containing a command.
MARITIME - Pertaining to the sea or to commerce thereon.
MARSHALING - Arranging or disposing of in order.
MAXIM - An established principle or proposition.
MINISTERIAL - That which involves obedience to instruction, but demands no special discretion, judgment or skill.
MISAPPROPRIATE - Dealing fraudulently with property entrusted to one.
MISDEMEANOR - A crime less than a felony and punishable by a fine or imprisonment for less than one year.
MISFEASANCE - Improper performance of a lawful act.
MISREPRESENTATION - An untrue representation of facts.
MITIGATE - To make or become less severe, harsh.
MITTIMUS - A warrant of commitment to prison.
MOOT (adj.) Unsettled, undecided, not necessary to be decided.
MORTGAGE - A conveyance of property upon condition, as security for the payment of a debt or the performance of a duty, and to become void upon payment or performance according to the stipulated terms.
MORTGAGEE - A person to whom property is mortgaged.
MORTGAGOR - One who gives a mortgage.
MOTION - In legal proceedings, a "motion" is an application, either written or oral, addressed to the court by a party to an action or a suit requesting the ruling of the court on a matter of law.
MUTUALITY - Reciprocation.

N

NEGLIGENCE - The failure to exercise that degree of care which an ordinarily prudent person would exercise under like circumstances.
NEGOTIABLE (instrument) - Any instrument obligating the payment of money which is transferable from one person to another by endorsement and delivery or by delivery only.
NEGOTIATE - To transact business; to transfer a negotiable instrument; to seek agreement for the amicable disposition of a controversy or case.
NOLLE PROSEQUI - A formal entry upon the record, by the plaintiff in a civil suit or the prosecuting officer in a criminal action, by which he declares that he "will no further prosecute" the case.
NOLO CONTENDERE - The name of a plea in a criminal action, having the same effect as a plea of guilty; but not constituting a direct admission of guilt.
NOMINAL - Not real or substantial.
NOMINAL DAMAGES - Award of a trifling sum where no substantial injury is proved to have been sustained.
NONFEASANCE - Neglect of duty.
NOVATION - The substitution of a new debt or obligation for an existing one.
NUNC PRO TUNC - A phrase applied to acts allowed to be done after the time when they should be done, with a retroactive effect.("Now for then.")

O

OATH - Oath includes affirmation or declaration under penalty of perjury.
OBITER DICTUM - Opinion expressed by a court on a matter not essentially involved in a case and hence not a decision; also called dicta, if plural.

OBJECT (v.) - To oppose as improper or illegal and referring the question of its propriety or legality to the court.
OBLIGATION - A legal duty, by which a person is bound to do or not to do a certain thing.
OBLIGEE - The person to whom an obligation is owed.
OBLIGOR - The person who is to perform the obligation.
OFFER (v.) - To present for acceptance or rejection.
(n.) - A proposal to do a thing, usually a proposal to make a contract.
OFFICIAL INFORMATION - Information within the custody or control of a department or agency of the government the disclosure of which is shown to be contrary to the public interest.
OFFSET - A deduction.
ONUS PROBANDI - Burden of proof.
OPINION - The statement by a judge of the decision reached in a case, giving the law as applied to the case and giving reasons for the judgment; also a belief or view.
OPTION - The exercise of the power of choice; also a privilege existing in one person, for which he has paid money, which gives him the right to buy or sell real or personal property at a given price within a specified time.
ORDER - A rule or regulation; every direction of a court or judge made or entered in writing but not including a judgment.
ORDINANCE - Generally, a rule established by authority; also commonly used to designate the legislative acts of a municipal corporation.
ORIGINAL - Writing or recording itself or any counterpart intended to have the same effect by a person executing or issuing it. An "original" of a photograph includes the negative or any print therefrom. If data are stored in a computer or similar device, any printout or other output readable by sight, shown to reflect the data accurately, is an "original."
OVERT - Open, manifest.

P

PANEL - A group of jurors selected to serve during a term of the court.
PARENS PATRIAE - Sovereign power of a state to protect or be a guardian over children and incompetents.
PAROL - Oral or verbal.
PAROLE - To release one in prison before the expiration of his sentence, conditionally.
PARITY - Equality in purchasing power between the farmer and other segments of the economy.
PARTITION - A legal division of real or personal property between one or more owners.
PARTNERSHIP - An association of two or more persons to carry on as co-owners a business for profit.
PATENT (adj.) - Evident.
(n.) - A grant of some privilege, property, or authority, made by the government or sovereign of a country to one or more individuals.
PECULATION - Stealing.
PECUNIARY - Monetary.
PENULTIMATE - Next to the last.
PER CURIAM - A phrase used in the report of a decision to distinguish an opinion of the whole court from an opinion written by any one judge.
PER SE - In itself; taken alone.
PERCEIVE - To acquire knowledge through one's senses.
PEREMPTORY - Imperative; absolute.
PERJURY - To lie or state falsely under oath.

PERPETUITY - Perpetual existence; also the quality or condition of an estate limited so that it will not take effect or vest within the period fixed by law.
PERSON - Includes a natural person, firm, association, organization, partnership, business trust, corporation, or public entity.
PERSONAL PROPERTY - Includes money, goods, chattels, things in action, and evidences of debt.
PERSONALTY - Short term for personal property.
PETITION - An application in writing for an order of the court, stating the circumstances upon which it is founded and requesting any order or other relief from a court.
PLAINTIFF - A person who brings a court action.
PLEA - A pleading in a suit or action.
PLEADINGS - Formal allegations made by the parties of their respective claims and defenses, for the judgment of the court.
PLEDGE - A deposit of personal property as a security for the performance of an act.
PLEDGEE - The party to whom goods are delivered in pledge.
PLEDGOR - The party delivering goods in pledge.
PLENARY - Full; complete.
POLICE POWER - Inherent power of the state or its political subdivisions to enact laws within constitutional limits to promote the general welfare of society or the community.
POLLING THE JURY - Call the names of persons on a jury and requiring each juror to declare what his verdict is before it is legally recorded.
POST MORTEM - After death.
POWER OF ATTORNEY - A writing authorizing one to act for another.
PRECEPT - An order, warrant, or writ issued to an officer or body of officers, commanding him or them to do some act within the scope of his or their powers.
PRELIMINARY FACT - Fact upon the existence or nonexistence of which depends the admissibility or inadmissibility of evidence. The phrase "the admissibility or inadmissibility of evidence" includes the qualification or disqualification of a person to be a witness and the existence or nonexistence of a privilege.
PREPONDERANCE - Outweighing.
PRESENTMENT - A report by a grand jury on something they have investigated on their own knowledge.
PRESUMPTION - An assumption of fact resulting from a rule of law which requires such fact to be assumed from another fact or group of facts found or otherwise established in the action.
PRIMA FACUE - At first sight.
PRIMA FACIE CASE - A case where the evidence is very patent against the defendant.
PRINCIPAL - The source of authority or rights; a person primarily liable as differentiated from "principle" as a primary or basic doctrine.
PRO AND CON - For and against.
PRO RATA - Proportionally.
PROBATE - Relating to proof, especially to the proof of wills.
PROBATIVE - Tending to prove.
PROCEDURE - In law, this term generally denotes rules which are established by the Federal, State, or local Governments regarding the types of pleading and courtroom practice which must be followed by the parties involved in a criminal or civil case.
PROCLAMATION - A public notice by an official of some order, intended action, or state of facts.

PROFFERED EVIDENCE - The admissibility or inadmissibility of which is dependent upon the existence or nonexistence of a preliminary fact.
PROMISSORY (NOTE) - A promise in writing to pay a specified sum at an expressed time, or on demand, or at sight, to a named person, or to his order, or bearer.
PROOF - The establishment by evidence of a requisite degree of belief concerning a fact in the mind of the trier of fact or the court.
PROPERTY - Includes both real and personal property.
PROPRIETARY (adj.) - Relating or pertaining to ownership; usually a single owner.
PROSECUTE - To carry on an action or other judicial proceeding; to proceed against a person criminally.
PROVISO - A limitation or condition in a legal instrument.
PROXIMATE - Immediate; nearest
PUBLIC EMPLOYEE - An officer, agent, or employee of a public entity.
PUBLIC ENTITY - Includes a national, state, county, city and county, city, district, public authority, public agency, or any other political subdivision or public corporation, whether foreign or domestic.
PUBLIC OFFICIAL - Includes an official of a political dubdivision of such state or territory and of a municipality.
PUNITIVE - Relating to punishment.

Q

QUASH - To make void.
QUASI - As if; as it were.
QUID PRO QUO - Something for something; the giving of one valuable thing for another.
QUITCLAIM (v.) - To release or relinquish claim or title to, especially in deeds to realty.
QUO WARRANTO - A legal procedure to test an official's right to a public office or the right to hold a franchise, or to hold an office in a domestic corporation.

R

RATIFY - To approve and sanction.
REAL PROPERTY - Includes lands, tenements, and hereditaments.
REALTY - A brief term for real property.
REBUT - To contradict; to refute, especially by evidence and arguments.
RECEIVER - A person who is appointed by the court to receive, and hold in trust property in litigation.
RECIDIVIST - Habitual criminal.
RECIPROCAL - Mutual.
RECOUPMENT - To keep back or get something which is due; also, it is the right of a defendant to have a deduction from the amount of the plaintiff's damages because the plaintiff has not fulfilled his part of the same contract.
RECROSS EXAMINATION - Examination of a witness by a cross-examiner subsequent to a redirect examination of the witness.
REDEEM - To release an estate or article from mortgage or pledge by paying the debt for which it stood as security.
REDIRECT EXAMINATION - Examination of a witness by the direct examiner subsequent to the cross-examination of the witness.
REFEREE - A person to whom a cause pending in a court is referred by the court, to take testimony, hear the parties, and report thereon to the court.

REFERENDUM - A method of submitting an important legislative or administrative matter to a direct vote of the people.
RELEVANT EVIDENCE - Evidence including evidence relevant to the credulity of a witness or hearsay declarant, having any tendency in reason to prove or disprove any disputed fact that is of consequence to the determination of the action.
REMAND - To send a case back to the lower court from which it came, for further proceedings.
REPLEVIN - An action to recover goods or chattels wrongfully taken or detained.
REPLY (REPLICATION) - Generally, a reply is what the plaintiff or other person who has instituted proceedings says in answer to the defendant's case.
RE JUDICATA - A thing judicially acted upon or decided.
RES ADJUDICATA - Doctrine that an issue or dispute litigated and determined in a case between the opposing parties is deemed permanently decided between these parties.
RESCIND (RECISSION) - To avoid or cancel a contract.
RESPONDENT - A defendant in a proceeding in chancery or admiralty; also, the person who contends against the appeal in a case.
RESTITUTION - In equity, it is the restoration of both parties to their original condition (when practicable), upon the rescission of a contract for fraud or similar cause.
RETROACTIVE (RETROSPECTIVE) - Looking back; effective as of a prior time.
REVERSED - A term used by appellate courts to indicate that the decision of the lower court in the case before it has been set aside.
REVOKE - To recall or cancel.
RIPARIAN (RIGHTS) - The rights of a person owning land containing or bordering on a water course or other body of water, such as lakes and rivers.

S

SALE - A contract whereby the ownership of property is transferred
from one person to another for a sum of money or for any consideration.
SANCTION - A penalty or punishment provided as a means of enforcing obedience to a law; also, an authorization.
SATISFACTION - The discharge of an obligation by paying a party what is due to him; or what is awarded to him by the judgment of a court or otherwise.
SCIENTER - Knowingly; also, it is used in pleading to denote the defendant 's guilty knowledge.
SCINTILLA - A spark; also the least particle.
SECRET OF STATE - Governmental secret relating to the national defense or the international relations of the United States.
SECURITY - Indemnification; the term is applied to an obligation, such as a mortgage or deed of trust, given by a debtor to insure the payment or performance of his debt, by furnishing the creditor with a resource to be used in case of the debtor's failure to fulfill the principal obligation.
SENTENCE - The judgment formally pronounced by the court or judge upon the defendant after his conviction in a criminal prosecution.
SET-OFF - A claim or demand which one party in an action credits against the claim of the opposing party.
SHALL and MAY - "Shall" is mandatory and "may" is permissive.
SITUS - Location.
SOVEREIGN - A person, body or state in which independent and supreme authority is vested.
STARE DECISIS - To follow decided cases.

STATE - "State" means this State, unless applied to the different parts of the United States. In the latter case, it includes any state, district, commonwealth, territory or insular possession of the United States, including the District of Columbia.
STATEMENT - (a) Oral or written verbal expression or (b) nonverbal conduct of a person intended by him as a substitute for oral or written verbal expression.
STATUTE - An act of the legislature. Includes a treaty.
STATUTE OF LIMITATION - A statute limiting the time to bring an action after the right of action has arisen.
STAY - To hold in abeyance an order of a court.
STIPULATION - Any agreement made by opposing attorneys regulating any matter incidental to the proceedings or trial.
SUBORDINATION (AGREEMENT) - An agreement making one's rights inferior to or of a lower rank than another's.
SUBORNATION - The crime of procuring a person to lie or to make false statements to a court.
SUBPOENA - A writ or order directed to a person, and requiring his attendance at a particular time and place to testify as a witness.
SUBPOENA DUCES TECUM - A subpoena used, not only for the purpose of compelling witnesses to attend in court, but also requiring them to bring with them books or documents which may be in their possession, and which may tend to elucidate the subject matter of the trial.
SUBROGATION - The substituting of one for another as a creditor, the new creditor succeeding to the former's rights.
SUBSIDY - A government grant to assist a private enterprise deemed advantageous to the public.
SUI GENERIS - Of the same kind.
SUIT - Any civil proceeding by a person or persons against another or others in a court of justice by which the plaintiff pursues the remedies afforded him by law.
SUMMONS - A notice to a defendant that an action against him has been commenced and requiring him to appear in court and answer the complaint.
SUPRA - Above; this word occurring by itself in a book refers the reader to a previous part of the book.
SURETY - A person who binds himself for the payment of a sum of money, or for the performance of something else, for another.
SURPLUSAGE - Extraneous or unnecessary matter.
SURVIVORSHIP - A term used when a person becomes entitled to property by reason of his having survived another person who had an interest in the property.
SUSPEND SENTENCE - Hold back a sentence pending good behavior of prisoner.
SYLLABUS - A note prefixed to a report, especially a case, giving a brief statement of the court's ruling on different issues of the case.

T

TALESMAN - Person summoned to fill a panel of jurors.
TENANT - One who holds or possesses lands by any kind of right or title; also, one who has the temporary use and occupation of real property owned by another person (landlord), the duration and terms of his tenancy being usually fixed by an instrument called "a lease."
TENDER - An offer of money; an expression of willingness to perform a contract according to its terms.
TERM - When used with reference to a court, it signifies the period of time during which the court holds a session, usually of several weeks or months duration.

TESTAMENTARY - Pertaining to a will or the administration of a will.
TESTATOR (male)
TESTATRIX (female) - One who makes or has made a testament or will.
TESTIFY (TESTIMONY) - To give evidence under oath as a witness.
TO WIT - That is to say; namely.
TORT - Wrong; injury to the person.
TRANSITORY - Passing from place to place.
TRESPASS - Entry into another's ground, illegally.
TRIAL - The examination of a cause, civil or criminal, before a judge who has jurisdiction over it, according to the laws of the land.
TRIER OF FACT - Includes (a) the jury and (b) the court when the court is trying an issue of fact other than one relating to the admissibility of evidence.
TRUST - A right of property, real or personal, held by one party for the benefit of another.
TRUSTEE - One who lawfully holds property in custody for the benefit of another.

U

UNAVAILABLE AS A WITNESS - The declarant is (1) Exempted or precluded on the ground of privilege from testifying concerning the matter to which his statement is relevant; (2) Disqualified from testifying to the matter; (3) Dead or unable to attend or to testify at the hearing because of then existing physical or mental illness or infirmity; (4) Absent from the hearing and the court is unable to compel his attendance by its process; or (5) Absent from the hearing and the proponent of his statement has exercised reasonable diligence but has been unable to procure his attendance by the court's process.
ULTRA VIRES - Acts beyond the scope and power of a corporation, association, etc.
UNILATERAL - One-sided; obligation upon, or act of one party.
USURY - Unlawful interest on a loan.

V

VACATE - To set aside; to move out.
VARIANCE - A discrepancy or disagreement between two instruments or two aspects of the same case, which by law should be consistent.
VENDEE - A purchaser or buyer.
VENDOR - The person who transfers property by sale, particularly real estate; the term "seller" is used more commonly for one who sells personal property.
VENIREMEN - Persons ordered to appear to serve on a jury or composing a panel of jurors.
VENUE - The place at which an action is tried, generally based on locality or judicial district in which an injury occurred or a material fact happened.
VERDICT - The formal decision or finding of a jury.
VERIFY - To confirm or substantiate by oath.
VEST - To accrue to.
VOID - Having no legal force or binding effect.
VOIR DIRE - Preliminary examination of a witness or a juror to test competence, interest, prejudice, etc.

W

WAIVE - To give up a right.
WAIVER - The intentional or voluntary relinquishment of a known right.
WARRANT (WARRANTY) (v.) - To promise that a certain fact or state of facts, in relation to the subject matter, is, or shall be, as it is represented to be.

WARRANT (n.) - A writ issued by a judge, or other competent authority, addressed to a sheriff, or other officer, requiring him to arrest the person therein named, and bring him before the judge or court to answer or be examined regarding the offense with which he is charged.
WRIT - An order or process issued in the name of the sovereign or in the name of a court or judicial officer, commanding the performance or nonperformance of some act.
WRITING - Handwriting, typewriting, printing, photostating, photographing and every other means of recording upon any tangible thing any form of communication or representation, including letters, words, pictures, sounds, or symbols, or combinations thereof.
WRITINGS AND RECORDINGS - Consists of letters, words, or numbers, or their equivalent, set down by handwriting, typewriting, printing, photostating, photographing, magnetic impulse, mechanical or electronic recording, or other form of data compilation.

Y

YEA AND NAY - Yes and no.
YELLOW DOG CONTRACT - A contract by which employer requires employee to sign an instrument promising as condition that he will not join a union during its continuance, and will be discharged if he does join.

Z

ZONING - The division of a city by legislative regulation into districts and the prescription and application in each district of regulations having to do with structural and architectural designs of buildings and of regulations prescribing use to which buildings within designated districts may be put.

Manufactured by Amazon.ca
Bolton, ON

24835263R10116